THE WINE COLLECTOR'S HANDBOOK

Storing and Enjoying Wine at Home

LINDA JOHNSON

FOREWORD BY MICHAEL BROADBENT

The Lyons Press
NEW YORK, NEW YORK

Printed in the United States of America

10 9 8 7 6 5 4 3 2 1

Design and composition by Rohani Design, Edmonds, Washington

Library of Congress Cataloging-in-Publication Data

Johnson, Linda (Linda J.)
    The wine collector's handbook / Linda Johnson.
      p. cm.
    Includes index.
    ISBN 1-55821-460-7 (cloth)
    1. Wine and wine making. I Title.
TP548.J664 1997
641.2'2—dc21   97-12779
                                      CIP

CONTENTS

ACKNOWLEDGMENTS vii

AUTHOR'S NOTE ix

FOREWORD BY MICHAEL BROADBENT xi

INTRODUCTION 1

1 WINE AND AGING 23

2 VINTAGES 43

3 FORMING THE COLLECTION 70

4 FINDING AND BUYING WINE 97

5 STORING WINE 119

6 SERVING AND TASTING 139

APPENDIX: WINE AGENCIES, INSTITUTES, AND
    GOVERNMENTAL ORGANIZATIONS 161

GLOSSARY OF INTERNATIONAL WINE TERMS 165

INDEX 187

ACKNOWLEDGMENTS

$\mathcal{I}$ would like to thank Peter Burford for accepting my book for publication, and Christina Rudofsky, for her constant assistance.

$\mathcal{T}$hank you also to Michael Broadbent for being an inspiration and role model.

$\mathcal{T}$o my colleagues in France who let me watch and learn and to the *vignerons* who let me taste and discover.

$\mathcal{A}$nd to Michael, my absolutely favorite cuvée spéciale, who lets me live, love, and libate!

AUTHOR'S NOTE

*T*his book is meant to be informative and practical. It is not meant to feed you subjective information about what and what not to drink, to buy, or to like, but to provide you with the information that will enable you to form your own opinions and develop and understand your own tastes. I hope to make you less dependent upon rating systems, vintage charts, and passing trends.

A second objective is to encourage you to do your own bottle aging, by demystifying the idea of aging wines. A wine collection, or a wine cellar, can be appropriate and beneficial for wines of all ages. A wine cellar that has wines of short- as well as long-term maturity dates will provide you more enjoyment, both sooner and later. By understanding how a wine is made, and why and how it ages, you can more easily create a cellar that includes a variety of maturation dates and fits your personal taste and budget. You'll learn which wines to buy for much later, for a little later, and for now.

I chose to use an international wine selection, because most of these wines can now be found through reputable merchants, auction houses, or mail-order companies. If this proves not to be the case for a particular foreign wine I discuss, try contacting a representative of the country in question. For example, the Wines from Spain office in New York City can provide a list of distributors that carry the bottle you are looking for, or the name and address of its producer, so that you may arrange either a visit or a direct order. (See the appendix for a list of such organizations.) Do realize that often, when it comes to small wine regions and producers, certain vintages sell out more quickly than others. If you have access to the Internet, this is a fabulous way to track down industry contacts. *The Wine Spectator,* for example, has a website that, among other things, will provide a list of wine merchants in your area. Don't hesitate to contact me at my E-mail address—lindawines@hotmail.com—with any questions or comments. I also have a website, (http://www.lindajohnson.com), on which I can construct a personalized wine collection for you. Come visit!

Note that, despite the rising popularity of New World wines (those from Australia, Chile, Argentina, the United States, and so on), serious wine aging (of ten years or more) seems to more often apply to the traditional Old World wines, simply because they have a track record. We don't quite know how some of the newer varietals from the newer regions are going to evolve. This is made even truer by the fact that in most cases they are intentionally made to drink while young.

FOREWORD

BY MICHAEL BROADBENT

*A*t last! A guide that is really useful, refreshingly direct, and eminently readable.

Perhaps I should not start with the style of the writing. Indeed, what is meant by style? And is it important? Easier to define what is not stylish: clumsy, disjointed, unattractive, lacking personality and depth. Happily, Linda has style, one that is both enthusiastic and relaxed; it is as if she is speaking to the reader and, moreover, speaking in a lucid and convincing way. I have enjoyed reading her book and hope you will, too.

But what about content? The first thing that strikes me is that it demystifies the entire process of selecting and cellaring wines—which, is, of course, the object of the exercise. It also does a little debunking of current myths: for instance, that the ordinary consumer cannot be trusted to rely upon his own taste, but must be led by pundits, the professional critics, some of whom espouse a basically flawed numerical rating.

Over forty years ago, during my formative wine trade days, I quickly learned that normal people inherently have good taste: that without any sophisticated knowledge of wine, customers—I was managing upmarket wine shops for Harvey's of Bristol at the time—could tell which wine was good, which was very good, and which was not so good. It was a simple subjective judgment, and almost always right.

Life, incidentally, was to some extent less complex for the importer and for the retailer then: Each was expected to use his own knowledge and expertise; indeed, his business would only thrive if his selections pleased his customers as well as himself. Nowadays every segment of the wine trade, from producer to consumer, is inhibited by the shadow of the critic: It reduces self-confidence and it has, I am sorry to say, emasculated the trade.

One of the most unfortunate results has been the fostering of an internationally acceptable taste: for example, red wines that are impressively deep colored, full of fruit, easy to taste—I call them plausible gold medal winners—as opposed to those that have subtlety and finesse, whose tannin content is less immediately agreeable in a pure tasting context but makes these wines better beverages (tannin is not only an essential preservative but also does a wonderful thing—it leaves the mouth clean and fresh between each swallow). Linda puts the case well: The New World is dangerously influencing Old World classics.

It is shortsighted folly for the ultimate goal to be a universally acceptable wine—like trying to breed a horse that is suitable for racing on the flat, show jumping, pony trekking, teaching children to ride, and pulling a brewer's dray (in London at least two famous breweries deliver casks of beer to their local pubs using carts drawn by massive Shire horses). "Horses for courses," I say, and so does Linda.

Perhaps I should add that Linda is uniquely placed to put the New World and Old World wines into perspective. She is an American wine writer and magazine editor who lives and works both in London and in Paris. She knows and understands the best of both worlds. Wine should not be taken for granted—but neither need it be put on a pedestal. Linda's book, engagingly entitled *The Wine Collector's Handbook*, is ultimately a thoroughly sensible, helpful, and down-to-earth wine drinker's guide. And always remember that wine is a civilized beverage, it pleases the senses, and, in moderation, it is good for you.

— Michael Broadbent
Christie's, London

INTRODUCTION

"*When it came to writing about wine,
I did what almost everybody does—faked it.*"
—Art Buchwald

ave. The mere sound of the word and my imagination runs amok.

And doesn't the French *cave* sound far more glamorous than simply *cellar,* evoking images of cavernous, humid, earthen cavities, dank with mystery? I picture myself as the châtelaine of a fairy-tale-style medieval château nestled in the French countryside, reposing in my sittingroom before a toasty fire, when Jenkins (all of my help is English, naturally) softly shuffles in and asks me if I care to choose a wine for the evening repast. We creep stealthily down the moss-covered stone steps, carrying Gothic candelabras, deftly dodging the spiderwebs. The heavy wooden door creaks open, and before me lie rows and rows of red-tinged oak barrels and alcoves filled with bins of every wine of every vintage ever produced—in unlimited quantities. I reach for my selections and make my way back upstairs to the dining room, where a twenty-foot-long, Christofle-laden table surrounded by eager guests awaits me.

Reality: I have a few bottles of Tickled-Pink in the refrigerator and two cases of other stuff in a closet somewhere.

While the fantasy of an authentic wine cellar is easily conjured, the thought of actually starting one is often daunting. Who wants to sink a small fortune into several cases of a succulent beauty from Pommard only to be told that he cannot drink it for at least another fifteen years? What's the point of having a cellar full of bottles that won't see daylight, much less your glass, until your fiftieth wedding anniversary? Isn't wine meant for enjoyment? It's understandable that eager wine lovers quickly grow impatient and frustrated when faced with the task of starting a wine cellar.

But what is important to realize is that "laying down," or cellaring, wine simply means buying wine in advance, laying it on its side, and letting it mature and mellow. It does not have to refer to an intricate, complicated plan that requires twenty years before it works; an operable *cave* can be achieved within months. (In French, the word *cave* is used primarily to mean the physical cellar, but has also loosely come to refer to the wine collection itself.) Both the timid debutante and the inquisitive amateur can accomplish this without having to spend a fortune, to travel the world over, or to possess an eighteenth-century vaulted cellar. Though the task of building a collection will be riddled with regrets (Maybe I shouldn't have dug the cellar under the septic tank?), the frustrations of hindsight (I should have bought more 1982 Bordeaux!), and confusion (Am I north or south of the Mason Dixon line?), the task is achievable.

The perfect collection does not exist. A "good" collection is one that represents different wine styles, wine regions, wine ages—and, most important, the personal preferences of the owner. And there will be mistakes. You should not be afraid to buy, however, nor should you sit around waiting for the "perfect" vintage. Remember—the worst thing that can happen is having to drink your mistakes!

WHY START A CELLAR?

There are concrete, practical reasons for starting to collect wines, and then there are the ones that are more abstract, or romantic. One of the practical reasons is the simple convenience of having a few cases stashed away and on hand. This keeps you from making costly mistakes due to hasty purchases or improper serving conditions. Pass by the local supermarket on the way home from work and you will find either an overpriced, young vintage not yet ready to open, or a bottle that is at peak maturation but far more expensive. Either way, you'll not have the choice you want, and you'll surely be disappointed. Then once you get it home, the chances of it having enough time to settle and to breathe are slim. Having a stock of wine you like readily available at home will ultimately save you time and money, not to mention the luxury of having a selection corresponding to your taste.

3

This alone justifies having a cellar. Add to it the intellectual enhancement and hedonistic pleasure your cellar will bring you, and the argument is closed. Isn't it far more interesting to explore your own personal taste, and to learn about a particular region, bottle by bottle, glass by glass? And isn't it far more satisfying to mature a wine yourself, follow its evolution, nurse it to perfection, and then share it with those who share your passion?

Another good reason to have a cellar is to help promote consumer bottle aging. Today, winemakers across the globe are confronted with consumers who buy for immediate consumption and competitors who put their bottles on the shelves as fast as they can. The system has become such a vicious circle that it is difficult to determine where it begins and ends. What and who changed first—the consumer or the product? It's becoming more and more difficult for producers to keep and age their wine in the *chais*, or winery storehouse, before releasing it. Those winemakers who are providing traditional, cellar-worthy wines are being run out of the race by the makers of easy-to-drink, inexpensive wines. There is a place for both of them in your cellar, and in today's marketplace. One should not exclude the other.

In today's international environment, with its global trends, wine quality is finding the lowest common denominator and so becoming more and more homogenous. We are witnessing the democratization of an old tradition whose craftsmen are being forced to adopt methods that don't suit their products. This has its advantages and disadvantages. The globalization of the wine industry, like all others, means that wine can now be enjoyed by more people, creating a mass market. And a mass market, although obligatorily expanding the definition of a product, is needed to sustain the product in its purest and most classic form. Wine is now accessible to those people who may never otherwise have entertained the notion of trying it. And once a certain acclimation period passes, the avid amateur usually begins to develop his or her palate, moving away from easy-to-drink, flashy wines and growing into the more complex and sophisticated wines. The objective is to ensure that while we use the more approachable wines to entice the novice, we don't lose sight of true quality and penalize those who are the craftsmen of the trade. It seems that whether it be clothing, cars, music—or wine—tastes are being dictated by a younger consumer who doesn't know the difference and who certainly is not prepared to pay for it. So while the globalization of wine allows for creativity, education, and profits, it also means risking the distortion and eventual demise of one of our greatest arts.

A BRIEF HISTORY

> *"Wine . . . cheereth God and man."*
> —Judges, 9:13

Venite apotemus!—"Come, let us drink!" A lot has been said on wine, whether extolling its virtues or lamenting its less pleasant effects. Wine, as the French gastronome Brillat-Savarin noted in his *La Physiologie du goût*, "goes back to the childhood of the world." And let's admit that it continues to nurture us, because mankind seems long to wean! This simple beverage is celebrated in song, poetry, story, and psalm, is obligatory in religious ceremonies and family celebrations, and is claimed as a cure for everything from hangovers to heart attacks. Wine has woven itself in and out of the history of mankind since the beginning of time: from Noah planting vines so as to have wine to celebrate the end of the long voyage on his Ark (Genesis 9:20) and Adam covering his private parts with vine leaves once discovering his nakedness, to the gods of Dionysus and Bacchus. Present in the literature of every major civilization—Egyptian, Greek, Roman—this sweet nectar has been titillating fancies and torturing souls for millennia.

And as much as mankind's history has been shaped by wine and its dizzying effects, so has wine's development been interlaced with the sobering realities of the economic and social changes to which we have been subjected since antiquity. For example, the Italian civil wars in 37 B.C. meant that Italians had to import most of their

5

wine for a while, thus accounting for the port of Ostia's plethora of amphorae from foreign countries.

The First Vines

Before the wine there is the grape, and before the grape, the plant. Throughout the world, most vine species orig- inated as indigenous weeds that grew wild for centuries and that were incapable of producing drinkable wines. Vine cultivation, however, is easily documented: There were various attempts on the East Coast of North America with the *Vitis labrusca*, in the Far East with the *V. amurensis*, and in Europe with the *V. vinifera*.

Time and again it has been proved that the *V. vinifera* produces the better wine. Planted vineyards have been found, indicating the plant's cultivation, south of the Black Sea in Transcaucasia dating from as early as 7000 B.C. Here, Soviet scientists have discovered at least sixty grape varieties belonging to the *V. vinifera* group—wild, but capable of producing wine. And wine containers found in Armenia date winemaking there back to 2000 B.C.

The art moved on to Georgia, whence it spread to the far eastern Mediterranean, including Egypt, where there still exist ancient illustrations of wine and its impor- tance in commerce and daily life. Then farther west through the ancient civilizations of Greece and into Italy, known to the Greeks as Enotria, or "Wineland."

It is said that the Romans introduced viticulture and vinification to France. What more likely happened is that the Romans stumbled upon a burgeoning local produc- tion center in southern France, probably in the town of Narbo Martius (Narbonne). Finding the wine there very good, they improved it with their know-how and were the first to market and export it, primarily back home—

for, prior to the Romans, a distinction has to be made between winemaking for private consumption and wine-making for trade and local commerce.

The First Wines

> *"God made only water, but man made wine."*
> —Victor Hugo, *Les Contemplations*

It is unfortunately impossible to know who might have been the first winemaker. Who initially noticed that a bucket of raisins left uncovered soon started bubbling and heating and finally turned into something rather agreeably potent? An absentminded monk? A lackadaisical laborer? At any rate, it certainly caught on quickly. The production and consumption of wine have varied (and continue to) through history to adapt to economic, political, and social structures—which, of course, change, collapse, and disappear. Throughout ancient history, the great civilizations took turns establishing cultural norms, copying each other, challenging each other, always competing (nothing has changed!). Sometimes all that was Greek, including their wine, was *à la mode*; at others, all that was Egyptian. Since 2000 B.C., popular preferences for wine have varied from watered-down vinegar to hardy, thick potions. We do know that men as well as women and children drank wine, and that all social classes drank wine, although not necessarily the same stuff: *Posca*, a mix of water and vinegar, was the common fare of Italian soldiers, and *lora*, wine diluted as much as one-fifth with water, was what Cato gave to his slaves. Much later, in France, château owners drank wine, while their *ouvriers* ("laborors") drank *piquette*.[1]

7

---

1. Andre Tchernia. *Le Vin D'Italie Romaine*: 10–18.

It is a common misconception that all of the wines of ancient Greece and Rome were drunk young. While it is true that most wines were sold and drunk within the year, there were exceptions. Very early in their history the Romans began making distinctions of quality and price.

These Romans loved rarity. They might have been the inspiration for Ricardo, the English economist, who in 1847 wrote: "There are things whose value depends upon only their rarity . . . such as precious paintings, statues, books and exquisite wines. Since we can only procure things from particular territories of very small scale and so by consequence, it follows that their quantity be very limited: no amount of hard work is able to increase their quantity." Early on wine was distinguished from other agricultural products, because its diversity was so much greater than that of, say, two kinds of beans, or several varieties of tomatoes.

8

"No man also having drunk old wine straightway desireth new: for he saith, the old is better."
—Luke, 5:39

Next came the logical tendency to oppose qualities. In wine, the obvious difference is between young and old. A young wine came to be defined as a wine of the current year's harvest. A good wine was one still drinkable a year later: A wine able to survive the hardships and heat of the summer season. The link between age and quality was established. As Diocletian wrote in his Edict, there was *vinum vetus sequentis gustus* ("good wine") and there was *vinum rusticum* ("rustic, coarse wine").[2]

2. Andre Tchernia. *Le Vin D'Italie Romaine:* 10–18.

In the first century B.C. the great wines of Italy came from the region of Campania, in which Pompeii is located. They were primarily white. Falernum, a wine from the Ager Falernus, and Caecubus, one from the Ager Caecubus, competed for first place, followed by wine from the Albin Mountains. These regions are known to have always produced very good wine, even before the terminology of growths was established.

Falernum was a wine of great alcoholic content. Pliny even claimed that it was the only wine that would catch fire—although I can't figure out why that would have been considered an attribute! The famous vintage of 121 B.C. was the first one described in Roman literature as first growth. The vineyard that produced this great wine was Falernum, and the wine was given the name Opimian, because Opimius was the consul that year. Caecubus wine, on the other hand, was very thick, sweet, strong, and intoxicating, with an amber color that took on the hue of fire as it aged.

It wasn't until the Middle Ages and throughout the Renaissance that a widespread preference for new wines was documented. In the early 1500s, wine would spoil as early as the spring following the fall harvest, dropping the price of a tonneau of old Bordeaux to eight times less than that of a vin nouveau. In recounting this paradox, André Tchernia, in his *Le Vin d'Italie Romaine*, explains that for some reason (perhaps due to a stronger northern European influence during this period?), winemakers started using tonneaux (wooden barrels) instead of the airtight, resin-lined amphorae for storage and transport. The amphorae allowed wine to ferment and age slowly, while the tonneau, much less impermeable to air, meant instant spoilage. This seems to be a step backward, and for two centuries was the law of the land, until the eighteenth century, which brought the start of modern winemaking, as we know it.

What held true then holds true today, only in entirely different proportions. Modern wine, for obvious reasons, is of better overall quality, and therefore better able to keep. The advent of the wine trade further promulgated this attribute: Traders needed to find ways to keep wine stable and transportable. Wines that were to be kept for months and years had to be concentrated and tannic so as to not spoil. (Much later in the history of the wine trade—the eighteenth century—we find winemakers adding alcohol and spirits to wine to "fortify" it, hence, the invention of port!) It was the attempts to conserve a wine for years, and to obtain an amelioration in the bottle, that led to the "discovery" of quality wines.

10

AMPHORAE: THE FIRST WINE CONTAINERS

For modern historians, tracing the history of wine consumption can only be done by examining remnants of the accessories left behind. There remain no wines, obviously, nor are there many original vineyard sites. But there are the containers—left in the holds of shipwrecks off the coastlines of the ancient ports—to help us to reconstruct the early wine industry and the habits of the first connoisseurs.

A classic, universal problem in wine storage has been finding a suitable container. Once our imbibing ancestors figured out that they needed airtight containers, they started looking around for an acceptable material from which to make them. This is where amphorae (Greek for "to carry with two handles") come in— ancient wine bottles made of terra-cotta that were easy to handle and easy to stack in ships' holds. Hundreds have been found off the coasts of almost every ancient Mediterranean port, as well as inland in France, Italy, England, and Spain. They are practically the only vestiges left of the ancient wine trade.

Why were amphorae made of terra-cotta and not glass, or wood? Economics, of course. Terra-cotta was inexpensive and available; most housing was made with it. Glass was considered too expensive, and impracticable for transportation, and so was confined to storing such domestic products as perfumes and oils.

Although the northern civilizations were storing their spirits in wooden casks, they could afford to do so. In Gaul, for example, the wooden *tonneau* had already replaced the amphora in the third century B.C. Barrels and casks were the special reserve of the Celtic civilization, where beer and mead, rather than wine, were drunk. The Celts devised this clever method of storage in which sophisticated tools and techniques were used to make efficient containers that were easy to handle and stack, as well as being lightweight and shock resistant—the very advantages that amphorae lacked. But the major difference, and the one the most difficult to assess, was the extent to which the container affected the taste of its contents.

Traditionally, the Romans did not use barrels. Julius Caesar discovered and described Gallic barrels in the Gallic Wars. Pliny the Elder pointed out in his description of Gaul in the first century A.D. that "methods for storing wine once it has been harvested differ greatly depending on the climate. In the Alps it is put into hooped barrels and in the depths of winter, fires are lit to prevent it from freezing."

Under the influence of the Romans, however, the Gauls started turning out large quantities of amphorae, which meant that barrels and amphorae existed alongside one another. Glass was still a rarely used luxury. Wine was

11

sometimes drunk from glass goblets, but bottles were not yet in common use.

Different-shaped amphorae were used to indicate the origin of the wine within: Italy, Spain, Gaul, or Rhodes. A wine amphora did not necessarily have a curved belly or pointed base. Unlike bottles, amphorae were not made for table use. They were solely storage and transport vessels, and so some had flat bottoms, particularly those used to transport wine from Gaul. During the Roman period, amphorae could contain between twenty and thirty liters. The amphora became, in fact, an official Roman unit of capacity, equivalent to twenty-six liters. Eventually, amphorae became the symbol of export activity, because whenever they were spotted being fabricated in a vineyard, it could be assumed that the wine was for export. Making such vessels for purely local consumption was unnecessary.

Amphora

In Italy and Gaul it was the wine merchant, or *mercator*, who purchased the grape harvest and then the amphorae needed, as well as overseeing the marketing of the product as a whole. Once an amphora was filled, care was taken to label it by providing information in either black or red paint. Information such as (1) the date the wine was "bottled," by mention of the Roman consul then in power; (2) the age of the wine, often referred to as *vetus* ("old"); (3) the quality of the wine, which might be *excellens*; (4) the grape variety; (5) the quantity of wine; (6) the wine's region of origin—for example, "White Wine from

12

Béziers" was found marked on an amphora discovered in Rome; and, sometimes (7) the address to which the wine was to be delivered. On an amphora from southern Spain, lost off the coast of Fos-sur-Mer, an address in Rome was given: "Roma in Via Lata," which corresponds to the present via del Corso, or the neighborhood adjacent to it.[3]

THE FIRST CELLARS

The history of wine storage, or the cellar, actually began quite a bit after that of wine. As we now know, the early winemaker went about the business of making wine for local consumption. It wasn't until he was approached by wine merchants who wanted to export his wine that he began to make his wine with a more commercial attitude. He noticed, for instance, that the merchants selected coarser, more tannic wines, and that they often asked him to mix his wine with warm must to concentrate it.

The first wines, then, contained in amphorae, were not privy to the same careful treatment they are offered today. If an early wine found itself in the ideal conservation environment, it was usually completely by accident. For example, the sea air and humidity along the River Thames in London kept the imported wines stocked along its quays from spoiling. Even before that, the Romans, those environmental engineers par excellence, stored all perishables, including wine, in *fumatoires*, smoke-filled rooms above or next to kitchens. The smoke preserved the wines—although, unfortunately, the heat from the kitchens often ruined them. The richest Romans had the luxury of devoting an entire *cella vinaria* to the conservation of wines, but they were still always on the

13

3. Fanette Laubenheimer. "Amphorae." *Vintage* 3 (Autumn 1995): 20–25.

ground floor. It would be interesting to know, in fact, why the Romans, so advanced in the domain of wine and temperature control, did not further develop this concept and establish more suitable storage standards.

The use of the first cellars was also limited to wine producers, merchants, and the noble or wealthy. In the major cities, such as Rome, however, the system of having a sort of makeshift wine cellar reserved for the rich was abandoned when the era of Roman villas fell, along with the Roman Empire. Before its tragic demise, Pompeii was a major grand cru wine-producing region. The wines were greatly sought after and exported all over the Empire. Apparently, Pompeii resembled Bordeaux in several ways: its role as supplier of the country's preferred and most sought-after wines; its status as a vast region of planted vines; and the presence of many great wine estates outside the city. Currently there have been found the remains of thirty-one villas—the châteaux of the era—of which twenty-nine were clearly wine-producing estates with extensive cellars.

The cellars of the notables in Pompeii, like those of their counterparts in Narbonne or Vaison-la-Romaine, were filled with a wide variety of wines from many countries. Recent studies of amphorae show that at the beginning of the Christian era, a small proportion of Italian wines, a large number of Spanish wines (especially from the provinces of Tarraconensis and Baetica), and some Greek wines from the eastern Mediterranean (Rhodes or Crete) commonly circulated in Gaul alongside the local wines.

The concept of a *cave* or a "cool" cellar is very modern, and is also a product of circumstance. Makeshift cellars of some sort were probably always built, but more likely intended as hideouts from attacking enemies, protection from storms, and repositories for stocks of grains, vegetables, and perishables. The construction of cellars did not

14

come into popular vogue until stone, rather than wood or peat, became the principal building material. Then architectural norms obliged each house to be constructed upon an arch (just as churches were built upon crypts), which provided the needed support (the earth, after all, shifts) and coincidentally created the ideal environment for conserving perishable goods. Digging only ten meters into the ground provides a constant 54-degree F temperature, with no seasonal variations—perfect for wine storage. And until the mid-1950s and the advent of electric refrigerators, this remained the best solution for storing and maintaining wine.

NEW WORLD VERSUS OLD WORLD

To what extent, you might ask, has the history of winemaking shaped and influenced today's wine industry and the palate of today's wine drinker? The answer: Enormously. Look at the difference between Old and New World wine and wine consumers. In countries with a winemaking tradition, wine is considered a cultural archetype—a structural and structuring element of culture—rather than a marketable good. Whereas nonproducing or recently producing countries—New World countries—have a completely different perception of it. Wine may represent cultural identity to a Spaniard, while in Australia it is a symbol of a person's participation in an alternative culture and lifestyle. In Europe wine is considered more a food than a beverage—something healthful and always consumed while eating. In the New World, however, it is an accessory to food, and a social activity. People drink wine before or outside a meal. And they may drink to get drunk, not to complement or digest their food.[4]

4. C. R. A. Neilson and Veronfiere. *Wine Tradition and Evolution*, (Paris: C. R. A. Neilson and Veronfiere, 1996): 180.

New World winemakers who are bravely and justly trying to acclimate consumers to moderate wine drinking as part of a daily routine have used the "food and wine" approach, making the pairing of food and wine a playful exercise. It is working—only a little too well! When in the past hearty and full-bodied red wines were the center of a European gustatory feast, now the food has taken center stage and the wine is asked to discreetly tiptoe around the roast pork and sauerkraut so as not to overshadow their personalities. Still, to effect any social changes, sometimes the pendulum must swing very far out before returning to a centered equilibrium. Thus the current popularity of light, easy-on-the-palate wines.

What is even more ironic is that some New World wines try to capture an Old World taste. The results, given the New World's warmer climates combined with overripening of fruit and heavy oak aging, are wines that have seductive, spicy, fruity first attacks but that lack structure and complexity, making their aging capacity near nil. These are wines meant for simple and immediate enjoyment.

Still, there is room in the wine market for the two "worlds." Individuality is as much an appreciated and marketable commodity as easy-to-drink, all-occasion wines are. The methods used to make traditional, ageable, quality wines are expensive and cannot usually be adapted to mass production and distribution. At the same time, in order to expand, an industry must please everyone—and right away.

The most important ramification of the globalization of wine styles is that, in order to compete in the New World market, the more traditional Old World wine producers must now take shortcuts in winemaking. They are trying desperately to find that magic balance of a wine that can be drunk while young—it must be fruity and spicy and oaky right away—yet has all of the structure and extracts needed to give it a long life. I think the two will ultimately be found incompatible—the compromise will mean a loss of quality.

The trend in both worlds seems to be for larger companies to produce a wide range of products to please all consumers. Smaller estates are having a harder and harder time, and many either close down, start producing downmarket products themselves to pay for their top-range wines, or join a group that markets their wine for them. Given such a situation, where does the amateur wine collector turn to find quality, ageable wines?

I firmly believe that, although there are different styles suited for different drinking situations, there are also "good" wines and "less good" wines. That there do exist objective criteria for describing and analyzing a wine. And that those who ask a young premier cru Bordeaux, for example, to be fruity, full bodied, and "accessible" (the new marketing buzzword) are asking the impossible. Something has to give. *A two-year-old, fleshy, fruity, and easy to drink Cabernet Sauvignon* should be an oxymoron, yet the phrase also describes the trend developing in Europe as wines of the Old World try to keep up with flashy, accessible New World products. European winemakers are now working toward wines that are—as one winemaker in Pommard recently explained to me—"smooth and softly tannic enough to drink now, yet complex enough to cellar and drink in ten years from now." Another friend, the director of a very prominent château in Bordeaux, assured me that adding sugar would make a wine ready to drink while new without detracting from its longevity. Something has to be sacrificed in this equation.

17

The Modern Wine Drinker

Added to the problem of *what* you buy is that of *how* you buy. How many times have you seen "Harriet and Bob" enter a wine store with a wine magazine in their hands opened to the "Buying Guide" pages? They choose their wine for the evening's dinner party based upon a wine writer's personal judgment. If the wine has received a store's or a guru's top rating, they ask no further questions. There is, of course, the argument that if you know absolutely nothing about wine, it may be preferable for you to consult an expert's, albeit a stranger's, opinion. But there are so many variables in wine drinking that this method's subjectivity should render it the last resort. For example, a California wine critic is not going to appreciate the same style of wine as a critic whose palate is used to French products. And even among critics with the same palate style, there are many different ways to judge a wine. A critic may be judging a bottle on its present structure and future potential (as is appropriate for a young vintage), or may be examining merely its immediate attributes (as for a wine at its apogee). It is also very important to taste each bottle individually, in the context of its origin, vintage, grape composition, vinification method, and the winemaker's personal style. Even within one estate a winemaker may create products originating from several different appellations and, within these appellations, from several different parcels of vines. A winemaker would be offended if these crucial details were forgotten or looked over. How do we know in which context a critic assessed a wine?

Even setting personal taste aside, don't forget that the same bottle of wine never tastes the same twice. A bottle opened in the home of a winemaker will not taste the same as it will at your dining room table. (Perhaps location alone accounts for that!) More important, in a professional *dégustation* a morning tasting will not give the same results as an afternoon session. Tasting results can also be influenced by foreign odors such as perfume, tobacco, and coffee; by diet (what the taster last ate or drank); by the taster's health; by the temperature of either the room or the wine; by the length of time the bottle has been open before tasting begins; and by surrounding noise and activity. All of this is compounded, too, by the natural life cycle a wine goes through after bottling. Taste a five-year-old St-Julien and you may catch it when the fruits are still present, or you may get it as it slips into its long, peaceful hibernation.

In the end, then, how important and reliable is an expert's advice to you if you don't know the details . . . and what assumptions have been made?

19

COLLECTOR VERSUS INVESTOR

Before you establish a cellar, it is important to know your intent. Are you planning on being a professional or an amateur—that is, an investor or a humble collector? There is a big difference. Wine collectors are wine drinkers. Wine investors are wine buyers. Wine collectors drink, while investors do a lot of talking. Wine collectors like a wine to be inexpensive and taste like it is not, while wine investors prefer expensive wines that may or may not be good but that may someday become more expensive. Mind you, wine collectors are perfectly aware that some wines require aging to reach their potential, and they are perfectly capable of restraining themselves from jumping on a bottle to drain it. But investors often find themselves at the other extreme—they may never even taste a wine at its apogee. Instead it passes through their hands, like a stock commodity, sold at the highest possible price. Perhaps it passes unto yet another gambler, or—with a little luck—perhaps into the glass of someone who knows to open and enjoy it before it's too late.

Wine investors are a completely different breed than wine collectors, alias drinkers. Anyone who is capable of treating a bottle of wine as an entry in a financial registry is, to me, a blasphemer. I tend to believe that buying wine for the sole intent of selling entirely misses the point. Investors are probably frustrated stockbrokers and bankers who wish to appear a little more well rounded and culturally aware. They probably *really* drink Scotch.

Other than the fact that it is a meticulous task that requires great attention and financial savvy, wine investing has hazards. Many find out too late that their "liquid" assets are not so liquid. Wine can be a smart investment, because its value can increase rapidly, but the risks inherent in such a venture make it less appealing as a money earner. The problems start with knowing what to buy, and finding a reliable source of advice is not always easy.

It is considered wise to invest only in the best vintages of the best-known estates, or in large, limited-edition wines. (Most of the wines we drink are not worthy of investment, because they are not famous or rare enough.) The object of the game is to obtain these wines as young as possible, which results in a mad rush to buy futures. It is preferable to purchase about eighteen months after the harvest of a particular vintage. This is risky, of course, because the wine is still in barrels. The best deals are made by purchasing futures in the first good vintage after several mediocre years. This will increase the bottles' appreciation, because they will be comparatively scarce. This practice will be discussed in detail in chapter 4. Don't forget, *anybody* with a large enough bank balance can call a local merchant and purchase all of the top-end "sure bets." But it is the discriminant collector, choosing wine according to quality and personal taste, who is the true connoisseur.

The largest problem with wine investment comes with selling, because it is generally illegal to sell alcoholic beverages without a license. So to whom do you sell that bottle of 1947 Yquem? If you are lucky enough to find a licensed wholesaler willing to buy your collection, you risk selling for one-third or one-half of the value of the wine, so that it can be marked up for retail. You can sell it at auction, but that is a very tricky business in itself. The wines that do reach the auction block are usually from well-known, established collectors or merchants. There is also no guarantee of the price at which they will be sold—and the seller pays the shipping costs and auctioneer's commission. In addition, auction houses such as Christie's and Sotheby's have very strict criteria concerning the condition of the wines they sell, and rightly so.

But I'm getting ahead of myself. This book is not for wine *investors*, it is for wine *collectors*. It is addressed to those who appreciate all styles of wine, but who also wish to encourage and participate in the preservation of wine and the craft of its making, and who enjoy and understand the process of the nurturing of wine—a living thing. It is for all wine lovers and winemakers who believe in taking their time.

21

CHAPTER 1

WINE AND AGING

"Wine can be considered with good reason as the most healthful and the most hygienic of all beverages."
—Louis Pasteur

WHAT IS WINE?

*B*efore you can judge a wine for yourself and esti-mate its aging potential, you need to know what it is and what contributes to its quality. The offi-cial definition put forth by the European Com-munity (n° 337/79, Annex II) is that wine is the beverage that "is obtained from the partial or entire alcoholic fermen-tation of fresh grapes (crushed or not), or from the juice of fresh grapes." Obviously, it is a little more complicated than that. But to define its physical makeup in the simplest terms, here is what we have: water (between 75 and 90 percent), alcohols, acids, polyphenols (coloring agents), sugars, car-bon dioxide, and (chemical) aromatic components. There are also many components of wine that we cannot see, smell, or taste: vitamins, proteins, amino acids, and so on.

For Great-Looking Legs . . .

Alcohol, that important element in wine, is produced during fermentation, when enzymes created by the yeasts change the sugar of the grape juice into alcohol, carbon dioxide, and heat. The proportion of alcohol to glycerin is what determines the limpidity or "body" of a wine, which we observe as "legs" or "tears." More alcohol and the wine is thinner, thus the legs run down the sides of the glass more quickly. More glycerin and the wine is thicker, with legs that drip down the sides more slowly. It is primarily the amount of ethyl alcohol that determines the sweetness of the wine.

For Vivacity . . .

The total acidity of a wine depends upon whether the growing season was too cold (grapes are overly acidic and underripe) or too hot (grapes are overripe). White wines generally have more acidity than reds. It is the amount of acid that is important: too little and the wine is bland and flabby, too much and it is vinegary. The right amount of acid, in balance with the wine's other components, makes it crisp, clean, and lively.

Tartaric acid is unique to grapes and to wine, and it represents one-third to one-quarter of a wine's total acid composition. Its content decreases as grapes ripen, and then varies depending upon the weather conditions at harvest. Tartaric is the strongest acid and strongly influences the pH of a wine—pH being a measure of the concentration of hydrogen ions, which for wine equates to dryness. The lower the pH, the safer the wine is from diseases and oxidation, and therefore the greater its aging potential.

Malic acid is found in every part of the grapevine. It is the most fragile of the acids and thus easily transformed into lactic acid. Called malolactic fermentation, this process diminishes considerably the overall acidity of a wine. The hotter the year's weather, the more quickly the acid decreases during ripening—which is why there is more of it when the weather has been cooler. All red wines are allowed to go through a complete malolactic fermentation. White wines can either go without, go partially, or go entirely through this second fermentation; it depends upon the juice's initial acid and sugar levels, and the style of wine desired. If a winemaker wants a crisp and green white wine, then the malolactic fermentation is halted or even not allowed to begin. For a buttery smooth white, the malolactic fermentation is permitted to continue longer or to complete itself.

Acids give a wine its shine or brilliance, especially tartaric acids, which renew the wine's color. It is the presence of malic acid that often gives a wine an apple smell. In the mouth, you can sense a wine's acid content by the irritation of your gums and inner mouth.

25

For a Lovely Complexion . . .

There are three sorts of polyphenols, or coloring agents. First are the anthocyanins, which are the red pigments in grapes that give red wine its color. The purple-red color of a young red is due to its rather unstable anthocyanin molecules, which, in the course of aging, fuse with tannins to change that color to ruby red. This polymerization of tannin and anthocyanin is aided by the dissolution of oxygen in the wine, which stabilizes the polymers. Second, phenol acids are present in the form of esters. The third, and the most important to aging a wine, are the tannins.

For a Long Life . . .

Tannins that are "condensed" are present in the grape; those that are "exogene" are procured from the wood during barrel aging. In grape stalks, skins, and pips exist tannins, which are released during fermentation and pressing to give a wine its specific character, and contribute to its aging capacity. Storing, or aging the wine in new oak, releases additional tannins from the wood's fibers. Exogene tannins can improve a wine's aging potential, complement its texture, and fill it out—but only if the wine itself has a solid backbone of acids, fruit extracts, and condensed tannins. Oak aging cannot replace raw materials that are lacking.

A wine's red color fades as its anthocyanins diminish with age. The more mature a wine, the more yellow or brown its "disk," or surface, becomes. The combination of these coloring agents can give the wine a sour taste and a drying sensation in the mouth, called astringency. The various tannins present in differently aged wines, and in wines from different regions, produce different sorts of astringency. For example, a young Bordeaux has tough and astringent tannins, while an old one has velvet soft tannins. The more tannins that are present in a wine's youth, the more it will make the sides of your mouth pucker, and the longer it will take to mature. Don't buy a recent-vintage Bordeaux premier cru and expect it to go down like velvet. That is what bottle aging is for.

For Sweetness . . .

Sugars are present in grapes, and each style of wine has a different level of sugar depending upon its grapes' maturity when harvested. Sweet wines contain several dozen grams of sugar per liter, while a dry white wine normally contains less than two grams per liter. The sugars, along with the alcohols as just mentioned, give the wine body and are visible in the legs formed on the sides of the glass. Sugars don't really have any odor but do eventually contribute to the overall expression of the wine. Also, it is the sugars that give the wine its sweetness, its fatness, and its unctuousness.

For a Bubbly Personality . . .

Carbon dioxide is the principal product (along with ethyl alcohol) of alcoholic fermentation. It is present in both still wines (only six hundred milligrams per liter) and effervescent. In the latter, carbon dioxide manifests itself as bubbles. It has no odor but is responsible for degaging the wine's perfumes, and in the mouth it has a bit of an acidic edge, pricking and tickling the tongue.

For Fragrance . . .

Aromatic components (chemical substances) exist in minus- cule quantities in wine and are issued from various chemical groups, alcohols, acid, esters, and so on. For example, the presence of ethyl acetate might make a wine smell like vine- gar; phenylethyl acetate like rose; ethyl caproate like soap; menthol like mint; and vanillin like (of course) vanilla.

What is important to note is that all of these fragrances are born of the wine itself—of its contents. Man-made manipulations, such as adding fabricated yeasts to the grape juice to jump-start fermentation, can be performed in order to rectify nature's flaws (low sugar, for instance, or high acidity), but they also alter the smell and taste of a wine. That is another book, however.[5]

THE DIFFERENT KINDS OF WINE

There are three basic categories of wine: table wines

5. Fribourg and Safati. *La Degustation* (Paris: Fribourg and Safati, 1996): 30–40.

(which can be red, white, or rosé, and either sweet or dry); fortified wines; and sparkling wines (which can also be red, white, or rosé, and either sweet or dry). Knowing how each wine is made will tell you what proportions of the above-mentioned elements are present in it and, logically, its aging potential. For example, red wines, because of their higher tannin content, last longer than whites; white wines with more acid and sugar last longer than lighter, less sweet white wines; and ports last longer than most red wines. There are no rules as to how much of each kind of wine you should have in your collection. It is really a matter of personal preference—although many people underestimate how much white wine they actually drink, or assume that all white wines are for early consumption and, consequently, run short.

Table wine is any wine that is still and not sparkling, and has not been fortified by the addition of brandy. Table wines usually contain 8 to 14 percent alcohol. Red table wines are always dry, whereas white table wines can be dry or sweet (botrytized)—witness Bordeaux's Sauternes, the Jura's Vin de Paille, Hungary's Tokaji, and Germany's Riesling Auslese.

Sparkling wine is any wine that contains carbon dioxide gas and 8 to 14 percent alcohol. It, too, can be dry, medium, or sweet. Almost every wine-producing region of the world has a sparkling wine. Spain has its Cava, Italy has its Prosecco and Spumante, and in France every region has one. Crémant d'Alsace, Crémant de Bourgogne, Vouvray (Loire). The most famous comes from Champagne and, of course, bears the same name.

Fortified wines can be dry, like a Spanish fino sherry; medium, like a Portuguese aged tawny port; or sweet, like a young tawny port or an Australian Liqueur Muscat. They contain 17 to 22 percent alcohol, since brandy has been added to make them stronger and more alcoholic.

How Is Wine Made?

As you've just read, grapes contain natural sugars, and their skins contain wild yeasts. When those yeasts come into contact with the grapes' juice, fermentation occurs. The winemaker helps this to begin by gently crushing the grapes to release their juice. This used to be done by foot and was called treading. (Do you remember that Italian grape-treading episode of *I Love Lucy?*) Unfortunately, this tradition is only observed now in some *quintas* in Portugal and in Greece. It is still the best way, but hardly economic.

For red wine, the crushed grapes and juice are placed into a vat to await fermentation. The process takes as long as it takes. If a winemaker feels that it will never start, he might add indigenous yeasts from the vineyard, or fabricated yeasts, to jump-start the process. Once it has begun the wine is run off into another tank, and the remaining extracts are pressed to release more juice.

White wines undergo this process in reverse: They are pressed first, and then the juice ferments alone, in a vat or cask. This explains very clearly the differences between white and red wines. It is the skins that give a red wine its color and flavor; the skins, pips, and stem that give it its tannins. White wine can be made from red grapes if they are pressed first—like the Champagne made from Pinot Noir and Pinot Meunier grapes, and the white Zinfandel made from Zinfandel grapes, which are red. White wines, even those made from red grape juice, have none of the tannins and less of the flavoring compounds of reds.

The crucial element of good fermentation is temperature: It cannot be too hot or too cold. Today most wineries are equipped with temperature-controlled electronic fermentation tanks. Once fermentation starts, however,

29

THE VINIFICATION OF RED WINES

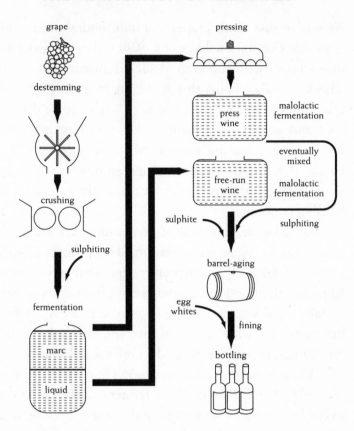

30

nature takes over. If the wine is too warm the must becomes too hot, the yeasts become lazy and inactive, and fermentation comes to a halt. It may restart if the wine is cooled down, or it may not.

When the wine has finished fermenting, it will look cloudy and have particles floating around, so it will be left to settle. After settling for a while, a sediment forms on the bottom of its container, or the lees. The wine is then transferred into another container (the process is called racking) several times. Finally, it is placed in barrels or tanks to age, which should serve to soften and develop it.

THE VINIFICATION OF WHITE WINES

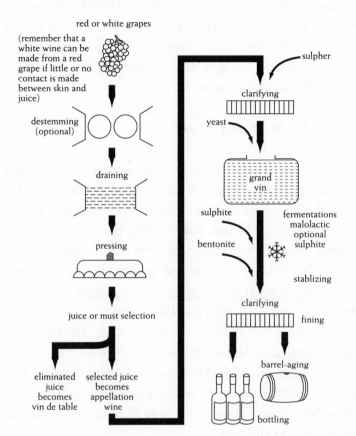

red or white grapes

(remember that a white wine can be made from a red grape if little or no contact is made between skin and juice)

destemming (optional)

draining

pressing

juice or must selection

eliminated juice becomes vin de table

selected juice becomes appellation wine

sulpher

clarifying

yeast

grand vin

sulphite

bentonite

fermentations malolactic optional sulphite

stablizing

clarifying

fining

barrel-aging

bottling

This is a very basic outline of how a wine is made. Describing the process of fermentation itself could fill an entire book, of course, but knowing the most important effects of fermentation upon the aging capacity of a wine is all that is necessary for intelligent wine collecting.

With red wines, for example, if the *cuvaison* (the period of time that skins and juice are in contact with one another) is too long the wine will become astringent and the tannins very drying and harsh; if the *cuvaison* is too short, the wine will be too light and thin, and it will lack structural tannins and aging ability. If the temperature of fermentation is too high the wine will have a cooked caramel taste; if too low the wine will not have enough color or structure. With whites, on the other hand, a high fermentation temperature renders the wine oxidized, unbalanced, and bitter. These are faults that will greatly cut the life span of a good wine!

WHAT IS MATURATION?

Assuming that everything has gone right up to now, wine will mature. In very simple terms, the maturation of a wine is a function of its composition, its origin (*terroir*), and its vintage. No two bottles from the same Bordeaux château but of two different years will develop and mature in the same amount of time. This is why the more you know of what goes into a wine and how it is made, the better you will understand how and why it ages.

There are two types of aging for wines. The first concerns fortified wines—those wines that owe their aging to oxidation, such as Madeira, port, and sherry. The second, and the one with which I will deal in this chapter, is the aging of wines kept away from the air—the fine red and white still wines.

This second category can be further broken down into barrel aging, which is part of the production process, and bottle aging, which some fine-wine producers undertake themselves before marketing their products, and which in any case is taken over by the eventual owner of the wine. This final step—bottle aging, or cellaring—is what happens while wine sits in your cellar.

No one knows for certain what happens during the aging process. We do know that the wine undergoes an olfactive evolution, however. The nose a wine has when it is young is called its aromas, while after it is oak aged

32

AGING CURVES

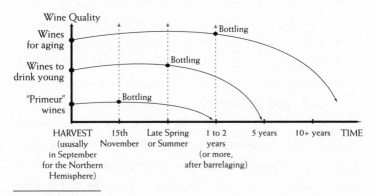

The moral of the story: The longer the wine is aged before bottling, the longer it should require bottle-aging before reaching maturation.

and mature these same odors become more complex and profound and are referred to as the bouquet.

During bottle aging red wines depose little plaques and grains of coloring agents and other molecules, which bond and fall to the bottom of the bottle. The heavier clusters settle faster and sooner than the smaller ones, which need years to settle. As these coloring agents settle in the bottles, the intensity of the wine's color diminishes, becoming first more reddish brick and finally yellowish, as the anthocyanins, or coloring agents, in the tannin soften and diminish along with those tannins.

When I say that the tannins "soften," what I mean is that the wine has reached a point of balance in its development curve. The harsh edge is taken off it, and its texture is smoother and less drying.

In general, the maturing of a wine involves four types of phenomena: chemical, physical, biological, and physical-chemical. Chemical maturation includes the oxidation of the polyphenols, alcohol, sugars, and organic acids; the conversion of alcohol into formaldehyde, acetate, and

33

ester; and, finally, the hydrolysis of polysaccharins and glucose. Physically there occur the insolubilization of salts, the release of gases, the evaporation of volatile substances, and the dissolution of tannins. Biologically we observe malolactic fermentation, which softens the malo acids, and a sort of funguslike enzymatic change for those wines that were wood aged. And finally (as if all of this didn't already n ake your mouth water) there are physical-chemical cl anges, such as oxyreduction, polymerization (the uniting of single molecules of the same substance to produce larger molecules, or mers), and the formation and flaking of colloids (substances that cannot crystallize and become solid, such as amidon and gelatin).

When Is Maturation?

Polymerization progresses continuously as the wine ages. Over long aging, then, tannic wines become gradually harder and more tannic, until they reach a peak where they are more tannic than they were in the barrel. Then the slope starts a gradual decline. The extra-large molecules lose their ability to combine with other proteins, and their astringency diminishes. At the same time they are combining with other components in the wine, becoming insoluble and precipitating to form the characteristic deposit. At this point the wine is in its mellow phase and is softer, richer, and rounder: This is maturity.

If the wine is kept too long, though, the increasingly large polymers gather strength once more—a sort of final wind—and become dry and astringent again. This is compounded by the fact that the wine is also losing its fruit and gaining volatile acidity. It is drying out, or dying. Knowing the moment at which to open a wine is a skill acquired, happily, through much practice! There do exist general

HOW A WINE MATURES

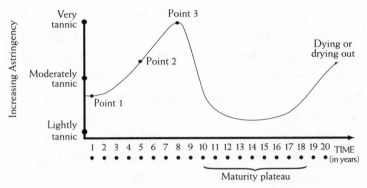

This graph reflects a wine's maturity curve, or the rise and fall of the tannins. The model is based on a classic Medoc of a good vintage. At point 1, the tannin molecules are not fully polymerized, and therefore the wine's texture is comparitively soft. At point 2, the tannin molecules are grouping together and forming larger molecules, and the wine has become more tannic and astringent. At point 3, the tannin molecules have formed one large molecule, and the wine is at its most bitter and astringent. Later, as the tannins start to soften (we don't know why), it becomes less astringent, and enters a mature stage, which should last as long as the number of years required for maturity to peak. After maturity plateau, it again starts to become astringent. It then begins to fade, dry out, and eventually die. You can tell an old bottle is dying when you can no longer taste its fruit and it seems very acidic. Note that the tannin levels at the maturity stage will always be less than when at point 1.

Source: page 3 of Michael Schuster's *Understanding Wine*, Mitchell Beazley, 1989.

guidelines based upon wine style and region; these are helpful, and I discuss them in detail in chapter 2. But the best guide is to always have a test case of a wine on hand, and to follow its evolution yourself by tasting it periodically.

Certain wines reach maturity sooner than others, and not every wine has the same length of maturity. In general, the duration of a wine's ideal maturation period is the length of time it needed to reach it, and the better the vintage, the later the wine will mature and the longer it will remain at its peak. If a 1982 Latour or 1982 Gruaud-Larose reached its apogee in 1997, then you can hope to enjoy your bottles for fifteen years.

Letting a wine mature means waiting for all of its components to fall into balance with each other. Maturing will allow a wine to develop its own distinctive complexities, rather than express a varietal character; *young* wines do that. A good wine is one that is balanced and harmonious. Its acids, alcohols, tannins, and fruits have all blended into one, creating a personality, a character. A less good wine will never fall into place, because its fruits will die; or its tannins will fade away into nothing instead of softening and holding the wine together; or its acids, the backbone and life of the wine, will become flabby or disappear. When tasting a young wine, look for all of these elements, to determine how well the wine was made and how it will mature. You can be rather certain of a young wine's character, but you never really know whether that character will endure until you test it years later.

36

Do All Wines Improve with Age?

No. Almost 75 percent of wines produced today are meant to be consumed young. This is a problem for a couple of reasons: First, there is the fallacy that all French wines, and even all Bordeaux, merit long cellaring. The truth is that the majority of French wine styles are meant to be drunk two to three years after bottling. Second, more and more producers, as I have already discussed, are making even fine wines that drink better when young, in order to compete with the lesser-known, lighter-style wine regions (barrel and bottle aging in the winery becomes an expensive luxury when your competitors get each vintage on the shelves before you've even finished vinifying), and to fit into the lifestyle of most wine consumers, who buy a bottle of wine to be drunk that same evening.

This said, I should add that even those wines not made for long hauls of ten, twenty, or thirty years would be better off with a year or two of peace and quiet. This gives them a chance to settle and regroup.

WHAT IS GREAT WINE?

Besieged by the marketing blitzes of all of those famous, expensive-sounding châteaux, don't you wonder what is behind their greatness? Should you strive to collect only the greatest wines, or settle for some of the ordinary ones, too? And how do you tell a good wine from a great? And what makes a great wine great? Should technical excellence take precedence over artistic expression? Should you revere creativity, or classicism? Do you commend effort, or merit? Do you demand qualitative consistency, or adapt to natural variations? Typicality or originality? Tradition or invention? Or is it strictly a matter of personal taste?

The answer: All of the above. Every one of these criteria overlaps onto the others until they become one and "great wine" is no longer possible to identify, dissect, or classify. A great wine is just grand. A great wine is one that responds to all of the technical demands of winemaking without losing its soul. It is capable of seducing without offense. It has the breeding and tradition that inspire deference, yet it continues its efforts to please. It is reliable but never boring. It reflects its origins without neglecting its individuality; it is the quintessential marriage of ancient and modern.

True greatness is a universal and unchanging concept. Despite changes in its definition, greatness itself has not been altered. Great wines do not bend at the will of consumer trend; they endure change and, in their timelessness, shape their epochs.

37

The Objectivity of Greatness

Indeed, how *could* greatness change, when the elements comprising it do not? Does a *terroir* lose its specificity? Do the rain and sun and wind so drastically alter their courses? Do mountains appear where once there were valleys? The scientific community might argue that minuscule physical evolutions do occur, due to erosion, pollution, genetic mutations, and general growing pains. I don't believe these are enough to make a significant impact on the wine.

The magic trinity of soil, climate, and grape variety must be considered the incontestable and objective determinant of a wine's quality. It has been proven time and again that a particular grape variety, when married to a particular soil, in a particular climate, produces a unique and specific result. We do not know why, but there are some grapes, soils, and climates that will never be able to produce a great wine, no matter what interventions man might offer to remedy the situation.

Which brings me to the topic of man and winemaking. What amount of responsibility should he be given? His influence is subjective, yet there are objective criteria determining greatness in wine. I would argue that man subjectively sets into motion these fundamental truths. Every step of winemaking, from planting the vines to bottling the wine, requires a decision that affects the quality of the outcome. It is no coincidence that wines born from those choices that are the most difficult and expensive to make are greater wines, and of greater value.

The Subjectivity of Greatness

Then there is the question of personal taste. Not everyone shares the same inclinations. Taste is an odd animal. For

38

although we do share inherent and permanent preferences at birth (for sweetness, for example), taste is also variable over time. To return to the wines of antiquity, we know that our Greek ancestors preferred spicy, resiny wines, and that early white wines were drunk oxidized and were rather acidic. But instead of insisting that this was because of the Greeks' collective taste, let's remember that this style of wine was preferred only by the general public, and that the average winemaker did not have the same wine-making techniques or capabilities that we do today.

And let's note, too, that a privileged class existed in Greece producing and drinking aged, bottled wines that more closely resemble our wines of today. Perhaps, then, it wasn't collective preferences that created the product, but the fact that the collectivity learned to like what was most readily available and easily produced. Who's to say that if a bottle of 1967 Romanée-Conti could have been made and tasted, it would not have been preferred to Retsina?

Is it safe to surmise that great wines are, by defini-tion, universally appreciated because of their classic con-struction? An analogy can be made in almost every discipline. For instance, almost everyone enjoys Mozart, while some may prefer the passion of Grieg; a preference for the latter, however, does not lead anyone to deny the brilliance of the former. This universal appreciation should not be confused with the modern phenomenon of vinicultural globalization, where the objective is to cre-ate a wine that appeals to all. The difference is that a great wine meets an unchanging standard and compels appreciation, whereas a less great wine caters to the taste of the majority and seeks a commercial and gustatory common denominator.

39

JEALOUSY AND CIRCUMSTANCE:
THE ORIGINS OF THE WORLD'S FIRST SWEET WINE

Hungary's sweet wines—the Aszú—can age for over two hundred years in a good vintage and are produced in extremely small quantities. They have been gaining in popularity since the East opened up. More and more foreign corporate investors (French and American) are buying up the old communist farms. The best Aszú, though, is produced by those farms that are still Hungarian owned and operated.

We owe the existence of Aszú to a vindictive village bureaucrat who, by intentionally stalling the 1649 harvest in the town of Tokaji, unwittingly facilitated the discovery of *Botrytis cinerea*, or noble rot.

This vague historical personage was jealous of the wealthy Rakoczi family, who in 1617 bought the property of Sarospatak and in 1647, the Château of Tokaji. The scenario is classic: a disgruntled government worker and an enterprising family dynasty. Throw in the impending threat of a hostile Turkish army and you have all you need to start the cameras rolling.

In the hope of thwarting the family's vintage, the civil servant ordered all commercial activity (particularly grape picking) to be halted so as to prepare for the supposed Turkish raid. It worked. But a few weeks later, by the time the villagers figured out that the Turks were not coming, little brown spots had developed on the grapes.

The family's winemaker, a priest named Maté Szepsi Lacko, picked what few grapes were still intact, blended them with a little bit of the dry white wine left from the previous year to try to play down this "problem," and let the mixture macerate until a second fermentation took place. The resulting must was thick and concentrated, with rich aromas and a golden color. It wasn't what the Hungarians were used to—but they liked it. Imagine the disappointment and frustration of our poor bureaucrat when he saw the family's riches double, and their name go down in history!

WINE AND AGING

The Secret of Tokaji . . .

Grapes that are fully botrytized make the wine called Tokaji
Aszú. In years in which climatic conditions do not favor
noble rot, the grapes are used to make the Tokaji wine
Szamorodni, which can be either dry or sweet. The unique-
ness of Aszú is due to its elaboration. After harvesting, the
grapes are stored in a *putton*, which can hold up to twenty-five
kilograms of fruit. They are not vinified right away, but are
added to 136 liters of dry white wine (harvested earlier and
sorted from the botrytized grapes). They are left to macerate
and soon start an alcoholic fermentation.

Tokajis are classified by their degree of sweetness. Using
the 136 liters of dry white wine as a fixed base, an increasing
number of *puttonyos* are added: between three and six,
depending on the quality of the harvest. The more *puttonyos*
of Aszú are added to the dry wine, the richer it becomes. And
in exceptional years, only Aszú grapes are used, creating the
rarest wine of all—Aszú Essencia.

Why German Sweet Wines Are Great for Cellaring

Of the twenty most expensive wines in the world listed
herein in this book (see page 115–18), notice that thirteen
are sweet dessert wines, and that eleven of those are from
Germany. This is a rather staggering percentage considering
that Germany only produces 2 to 3 percent of the world's
wine! As in all sweet, or late-harvest (noble rot), wine-
producing regions, the Germans harvest grapes at various
stages of ripeness (selective harvesting), in order to establish
the quality category of a wine.

What do all of these wines have in common? Their great
capacity to age and mature. Among all of the factors contributing to a wine's aging capacity, the balance of acid and
the right kind of tannins is crucial for reds, while the amount
of acidity is key for whites. A Beaujolais Nouveau will never
be a great wine; neither will a dry Muscadet.

And although the Hungarians claim to have discovered
Botrytis cinerea, or noble rot, in 1649 (see "Jealousy and

41

Circumstance" on p. 40), the Germans claim to have discovered it in 1775! As the story goes, the monks at the vineyards of Schloss Johannisberg, who never started harvesting without the permission of the Abbot of Fulda, began to panic when they detected brown rot on some of their grapes. The Abbot had not yet returned from a voyage, so they sent a messenger to him. By the time the messenger returned the monks thought the harvest was lost, but they went ahead with it anyway. Or course, they loved the wine, and everyone lived happily ever after.

TBA or Not to Be!

Germany's northern location provides a moderate climate without intense heat, so grapes take longer to fully mature than in warmer climates. German wine harvests therefore take place in October and November. However, the time of the picking is not as important as the ripeness of the grape at harvest. This ripeness is indicated on the label by a quality category. Under German wine law there are two categories of quality: Tafelwein ("table wine"), and Qualitätswein ("quality wine").

Qualitätswein mit Prädikat ("quality wine with special distinction") is the category that includes all of the finest wines of Germany. It is further divided into six quality categories:

Kabinett—light, semidry wines made from normally ripened grapes.

Spätlese—from *spät* ("late") and *lese* ("picking"). These are wines from grapes picked after the normal harvest.

Auslese—meaning "outpicked." Wine from selected, very ripe grapes.

Beerenauslese—from *beeren* ("berries"), *aus* ("out"), and *lese* ("picking"). Wine from grapes that are individually picked.

Eiswein—or "ice wine," wine made from grapes of the same level of ripeness as the Beerenauslese, but harvested and pressed while still frozen.

Trockenbeerenauslese (TBA)—wine from grapes that are overripe and dried up like raisins. These grapes produce the richest, sweetest, and most expensive wines.

VINTAGES

"A fine wine lasts a long time in your
mouth . . . and in your mind."
—Christian Moueix,
Director of Château Petrus

hy does a bottle of wine bear a year, or vintage? *Vintage* refers to much more than a wine's age; it is the date given to a particular year's grape harvest. The vintage is extremely important in the evaluation of a wine's quality and cellaring potential, because the climatic conditions of a particular growing season directly affect the wine's structure and, therefore, its capacity for maturation. Vintage is thus an identification of quality and can be considered a code for a wine's structure and the way in which it will develop. A dry, overly hot summer, for example, might mean a high alcohol content; heavy rains at the time of harvest can cause dilution and light fruit extraction. Both are impediments to a long life.

Many wine collectors thus rely upon vintage charts first to decide which wines need cellaring, and later to decide when the wines are ready to drink. A vintage chart is a grid matrix with wine regions or countries used as the coordinates of one axle, and vintage years of the other.

Where a region connects to a vintage is a rating—good, bad, or excellent, for instance, or whatever scale of measure the author has chosen to use. The problem with vintage charts and vintage ratings is that there are always exceptions to the rule. They should be considered only guidelines. For the greenest wine debutante they are good starting points—they are better than nothing. But it is interesting, and sometimes necessary, for collectors to dig more deeply. Most vintage charts are too broad: They cover an entire wine-producing area, brushing over the dozens of microclimates that exist within it and ignoring the variables that make up a vintage's potential. Some even argue that vintage years are less important, or less indicative of quality, in New World wines, because the climates of California, Chile, Australia, and so forth, are not as variable as their European counterparts. Napa seems to always be either sunny or sunnier!

This said, one of the best international vintage charts I have come across is Robert Parker's *The Wine Advocate's Vintage Guide*. He breaks it down by country and region or grape variety, and has a complex yet clear system of symbols denoting a vintage's quality and aging potential (most charts just note current quality). For example, he notes in his 1970–1993 *Guide*, dated February 26, 1995 (he is even careful to let you know when his notes/tastings were completed), that the 1988 northern Rhône, Côte Rôtie, is rated *92E* in bold type; meaning that 1988 is a top vintage, that he rates it a 92, or the finest, and that *E* denotes an early maturing vintage. He also adds that vintage charts should be used as a "very general overall rating of a particular viticultural region . . . filled with exceptions to the rule . . . astonishingly good wines from skillful or lucky vintners in years rated mediocre, and thin, diluted, characterless wines from incompetent or greedy producers in great years . . ." I could not have said it better myself.

Another exception to the rule, the leading French wine magazine, *La Revue du Vin de France,* publishes their *Guide de la Cave* once a year, and includes maturity projections for *each* Bordeaux château and Burgundy appellation, as well as the top Rhônes! It is extremely detailed and useful, and I can personally vouch for the skill and expertise of the magazine's tasting panel.

What happened one year in Burgundy or Napa may not be true in corresponding microclimates of Meursault or Rutherford Bench. Meursault is only a small part of the Burgundy region, and a typical vintage chart will not take this into consideration. Nor will it differentiate between red and white wines, never mind the different grape varieties of red and white. Perhaps the Merlot and Chardonnay were harvested under sunny skies, for example, but by the time the Cabernet Sauvignon came in the vines were drenched by a late summer storm. And to get even more microeconomic: Most vintners bring in their best grapes first, rather than risk foul weather. This means they bring in their grand cru or premier cru parcels first, and tend to their lesser parcels afterward. This sounds really nitpicky but I promise that you can taste the difference—and certainly you pay for the difference.

45

Recently, on a tasting trip to a large estate in Burgundy, I did a horizontal tasting of a vintage that had experienced two periods of rain in September, the first (and much lighter) occurring near the 12th, the second near the 21st. Burgundy was divided between those winemakers who brought their grapes in before or after the first rain, and those who took the risk and got caught up in the second. When I compared two different bottles issued from two different parcels of the same estate, the one harvested later under rainy skies was lighter and less acidic. There was an obvious difference in concentration between the two—and consequently there was a price difference of nearly 50 percent—a perfect example of how a vintage chart can be correct and incorrect within a single estate's production.

Another thing to watch for is the origin of the vintage chart. Look for hidden biases. Who wrote it—the local winemakers' committee or regional press office? Probably. Charts from such sources are almost invariably noncommittal. Have you ever noticed how all of the vintages on these charts are listed as "excellent," "very good," "good," or "average," but never "bad"?!

Even if a vintage chart is truly objective and rates a particular vintage as disastrous, it is still too subjective. For though some years may be worse than others, it is a crime to disregard an entire year's production of wine because of such a judgment. There will always be a little pocket of vines, or an estate, or a particular grape variety, that did better than the rest. Condemning the entire lot is what can put small wineries out of business.

What does it mean if a wine label does not indicate a vintage year? Simply that the wine in that bottle is from grapes of different years. Maybe the winemaker mixed some of a previous year's wine with the current year's must. There are a lot of reasons for doing this, some of them good. To play it safe, however, know that this is not the mark of a serious wine for cellaring, and avoid it. But note also that by law, a vintage-marked bottle must contain 75 percent (or 85 percent, depending upon the country and wine-quality designation) of that particular year's harvest. It is perfectly legal, and qualitatively acceptable, to top up a vat with a little of last year's wine.

How to Analyze a Wine's Potential

It is the appellation—or, more specifically, the *terroir*—of a wine, in conjunction with its vintage year, that ultimately determines its extraction and density, and therefore its aging potential. There are no shortcuts. It all starts at the dawn of the new year, with the first ray of sunshine. Every drop of rain or dose of sun can alter the route from bud to grape to bottle. This can become extremely complicated, but if you understand as much as you can about the life cycle of the vine and the influences of the climate, you can start making your own conclusions about vintages and complement the use of vintage charts with them. Of course, it would be unrealistic to expect to know every year of every region—that takes a lifetime and is a job in itself—but if you have a favorite wine region, say Chablis, or Tuscany, or Hunter Valley, it might be enjoyable and interesting to follow it closely and get to know it.

47

Most enological/biological studies have been based upon the traditional European climate models. But noble grape varieties such as Chardonnay and Cabernet Sauvignon are today grown in almost all wine-producing regions of the world, and their growing seasons are altered by the local climates of these faraway places. Still, the European model can, and should, be used as a guide. Actually, this is a major topic of debate: Should the noble varieties be transported from their home soil and climate? And when they are, how is their lineage affected? The answer becomes clear once you taste a Cabernet Sauvignon or Pinot Noir from a warm-weather region and one from its native Bordeaux or Burgundy.

Warm climates shorten the growing season, which ripens the fruit more quickly—but without letting it achieve the same maturity of flavor development found in cooler-climate fruits, which were nurtured longer by the vine before being harvested. This is called the hang time, and the longer it is, the better. Slow-ripening fruit becomes more complex and sophisticated, thereby guaranteeing a later, yet more sophisticated and longer-lasting maturity.

A short growing season translates into wines that have fruity first attacks with good primary extractions, but little acid for structure and no complexity. Think of a thirteen-year-old girl dressed up in her mother's high heels and lipstick: She may look ripe on the outside, but the content is perhaps rather thin and simplistic. The wines then dry up and fade away, leaving only alcohol and harsh tannins. These will always be very unbalanced wines, for balance manifests itself one way or another and signs of it are evident even when a wine is young. If it's not there at the start, it won't be there later on.

Gathering as much information as you can about a wine—its grape(s), maker, and origin—will aid you in determining what you should expect from it and, more important, what it will deliver later.

FROM BUD TO BOTTLE

The analogy made above between a young girl and wine who both reached false adulthoods too quickly can be carried even further. The girl's personality and character are in large part formed by her early experiences, be they physical or emotional. The same can be said of wine. It is by examining its heritage (genetic history or subjective influences) and environment (external influences) that you can pretty much judge its character and physical makeup—and, thus, its aging potential.

Although the winemaker cannot greatly influence a grapevine's genetics (I won't go into a discussion of cloning, of rootstock selection, of hybrids, etc., for it is a topic that merits a book unto itself and that confuses me terribly), decisions are made concerning its environment that will have very long-reaching effects. Here is a very brief description of what a grape has gone through before it is picked.

After the harvest, which in the Northern Hemisphere is usually during the month of September (except for sweet white wines), the vine closes down for the winter, but comes back to life with the first rays of sunshine. The recently pruned branches, or canes, glisten with syrupy tears of sap. Then, near February, little furry buds develop on the knob of each cane. At the first sign of spring, usually in April, these buds begin to open (the process is called budburst, or *débourrement*), and tender little cabbage-like heads of green leaves appear, in the middle of which are nestled minuscule bunches of grapes. This stage is slow moving, but speeds up as soon as the air reaches a constant warm temperature. This is the most delicate period of the vine's life—the time when it is most vulnerable to sudden spring frosts, which can freeze entire crops.

In June, when the air temperature reaches about 70 degrees F, comes the flowering, or *floraison*. Early flowering is considered a sign of a good vintage. But if the weather is too cold during flowering, the grapes may not develop properly. During this period the vine needs long days of sunshine while it pollinates. The berry starts to take shape—this is called setting—and, if all goes well, it quickly becomes larger and heavier. Once it reaches the height of its development, it changes from its green color to either a transparent yellow (if it's a white grape) or a deep violet (if red). Called the *véraison*, this change usually happens in the summer. The grapes fill up with sugar and water, becoming fully mature, and await harvest.

49

What Can Go Wrong

The weather conditions that pose the greatest threat to a maturing vine are winter and spring freezes, hail, rain, and extreme cold or heat waves. A winter freeze is especially dangerous if the temperature drops below −15° C. While unusual, this can cut a harvest in half. (A light layer of snow can actually help to protect or insulate the vines from stagnant freezing air.) A spring frost is even more dangerous, because the plant is just opening up and is at its most vulnerable stage. Such a frost usually sneaks in during clear, calm nights, when the temperature may drop to 30 degrees F. If it happens on an evening when there are clouds in the sky and a little wind, the danger is minimized: The wind creates a little turbulence, drawing heat from the ground, and then the clouds retain this heat. Have you seen winemakers trying to ward off spring frosts by burning brush or rubber tires among their vines? It is to ward off freezing.

Hail is most dangerous after *floraison*, when the newly formed grapes can be shattered (known literally as a "shatter") and broken. Rain during *floraison* can cause *millerandage*, which is a partial form of shatter and prohibits the plant from blooming. The flowers are pollinated but not yet impregnated, which means that they won't acquire pips, but will remain small and green. Uneven development can thus occur within the same bunch. Too much rain also means too much humidity and a greater chance of rot and mildew attacks. And rain at harvesttime, once grapes are mature, means swollen, watery fruit and diluted wine. This is why knowing when to harvest is so important. A perfect growing season can be ruined by a last-minute September rain, which will ruin the health and concentration of the grapes, and by extension the wine's aging potential.

THE LIFE CYCLE OF A WINE

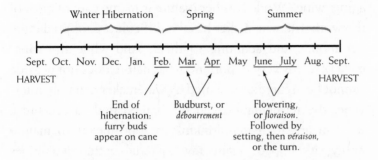

Note: This chart is based upon the classic model as practiced in France. In the Southern Hemisphere it would be the opposite, but the same principles apply.

The same is true of dryness and heat. A winter that is too warm will allow a precocious budburst, which will leave the plant too vulnerable to spring frosts. And a sudden heat wave in August or early September can block the maturation process and create overly acidic, tannic wines.

So what would be an ideal season? A winter sufficiently humid to reconstitute the plant's reserves yet cool enough to avoid an early budburst. Spring should be rather warm, so that the budburst is rapid. This allows a rapid vegetative maturation, which then protects the plant from parasite attacks. And, of course, there should be no frosts.

Late spring (May and June) should be warm and dry with no rain. Summer should be even warmer and dryer, to allow a good *véraison* and a good concentration of sugars, both of which help the plant to continue fighting off parasite attacks—although too much heat, as I mentioned earlier, means too much sugar and a high level of alcohol. This combination kills the future wine's finesse.

51

THE WINEMAKER'S YEAR

What can a winemaker do to make a better, and longer-aging, wine? While Mother Nature is taking care of most of the work, the winemaker has the difficult task of predicting her moods and adapting to them. And while the wine-maker's role is very important, what nature does not provide cannot be created or invented. A winemaker can only inter-vene, the fermentation can be manipulated to procure a wine meant for early drinking, or one meant to mature nobly (it's hoped, again, raw material better determines that). What follows is a simplified account of how a wine-maker can best aid the potential and quality of the harvest.

October. The harvest is usually over and it is time to pre-pare the soil, clear the ground, and/or replant. In the winery, vinification of the current harvest process begins.

November. The preparatory pruning is started, a prelude to the more crucial spring pruning. The branches are cut, and all useless shoots at the base of the vine are removed. The point of pruning is to prevent too many grape bunches from appearing per plant, which would dimin-ish yields. (Nature is very elitist: Grapes receive better attention if they are sparse than if they're part of a mass—another analogy to life.) Hilling up is also com-pleted. This means that the soil is prepared for the possibility of winter frost, and the base of the vine is pro-tected. In the winery, those wines that will be sold as "nouveau"—such as the Beaujolais Nouveau—are already being bottled.

December. The winemaker continues hilling up, soil replacement, preparatory pruning, and cane burning

(burning of dead branches). In the winery, the most important work now is maintaining the temperature of the vinifying wines so that their alcoholic and malolactic fermentations go well. (Not too hot, too cold, too fast, too slow . . .).

January is a quiet month in the fields. Pruning can be done, if necessary, but otherwise it is preferable to wait until February. Things are also a little calmer in the winery; the principal activities are watching everything cook away and topping up (mixing the thick top layer of skins with the grape juice).

February means major spring pruning, which has as its objective the direction, regulation, and improvement of the vegetation and fruiting of the vine. The winery is busy with general housekeeping chores—preparing the barrels and equipment and more topping up.

53

March. Fertilizers (if used) are spread in the vineyard: nitrogen for the vegetation, phosphoric acid for the fruiting, and potassium to increase yields by giving the grapes more sugar and less acidity. The more fertilizer is used, the more grapes the plant will produce and, therefore, the higher the yield. By the same token, controlling the dosage of fertilizers is, along with pruning, a way to curb yields. This is also the appropriate time to graft vines if they have fallen victim to phylloxera; this joining of a weakened cane to a healthy one is usually completed in two or three weeks. Basic gardening chores are also attended to in March: weed killing, airing the soil and plant, and so on. The work in the winery is equally important. Wines meant for early consumption have finished their fermentations, undergone sulphiting, stabilization, fining, and clarification, and are now ready to be bottled.

April. The plants have begun to grow and it is time to fasten them to the bottom wire, horizontally, so that new shoots grow vertically. In the winery, those wines not already bottled have begun their *élevage*, or maturation period.

May is when the plants are most vulnerable. Weed killers are applied continually, and treatments are begun to ward off parasites and fungi responsible for mildew and oidium. The lookout for spring frosts is also under way. In the winery, the wines continue maturing.

June brings more treatments, soil disinfection, and *accolage*, or the tying up of the vertical vine shoots. Normally, these will have reached the second and third horizontal wires by now. *Rognage*, or "trimming," is also completed. This thins the vine out, giving the grape bunches better exposure to the sun.

July and August are spent surveying the temperature and watching for possible parasite and disease attacks. The vines are carefully trimmed and tended. In the winery the preparatory tasks for the upcoming harvest have begun: the cleaning of tubs, casks, vats, pressers and crushers, pumps, and motors.

September. In both fields and winery comes the harvest. At the beginning of the month the winemaker starts regularly testing the grapes' sugar levels in order to determine the best date to pick. Grapes are harvested either by hand or by machine, brought into the winery, and sorted, eliminating all branches, leaves, and rotten or immature grapes. They are destalked and destemmed, either partially or entirely, depending upon the vintner's preference. Then they are crushed, pressed, and sent on their way to start their fermentation.

This is a crucial month. Assuming that the winemaker started with the correct rootstock of a noble grape variety, planted it in a suitable soil, enjoyed clement weather conditions throughout the year, and provided maximum pruning and care coupled with only the most necessary technical interventions, the decisions made now will further determine the wine's final character and potential: whether to handpick the grapes, and how much of the pips and stalks to leave in during fermentation (in other words, how much extract the juice can take). Remember, the skins, stalks, and pips of the grape contain the tannins, and the winemaker has to perfectly measure each ingredient of the recipe in order to obtain a balanced, well-made result.

The Harvest Report

A harvest report is usually prepared by a journalist or a wine trade professional for a trade journal or a wine-industry regulatory body. For example, in Burgundy, France, the BIVB (Bureau Interprofessionnel des Vins de Bourgogne) oversees, coordinates, and promotes the region's wine industry. It might release to the press and public its own estimation of a particular vintage based on the year's weather patterns and the crops' condition. You can obtain this raw data and study it yourself, or read professional analyses of it, which are published in trade and specialist magazines.

The goal of a harvest report is simply a rational analysis of a wine's structure—a determination of whether its tannin, acid, alcohol, and fruit will make a balanced future wine. This is not always easy to do. If the reporter is sampling barrels in Pommard only six months after harvest, for instance, he or she will get a mouthful of tannins and have a hard time tasting anything else. Harvest reports as an observation of a year's growing season are valid; as a prediction or guarantee of quality they are less so. Still, the exercise can be helpful.

Below are some brief summaries of harvest reports. Although you may consider them boring reading, they do illustrate the importance of knowing details of a vintage's growing season, as well as how a professional taster goes about things. Perhaps they will help you make your own evaluations and judgments, according to your taste.

I chose to include California 1994 and Burgundy 1993 only to better illustrate the differences in wine language. Where the Californian is worrying about low acids, the Burgundian frets over low sugars and contemplates chaptalization, an illegal practice to the former . . . and so it goes on. The often opposing attitudes toward yields, temperature and climatic variations, etc., are also clearly evidenced.

Analyzing a Vintage: California 1994

California may be a difficult place to start this survey, because the very idea of differentiating among California vintages has often been ridiculed. The seemingly unchanging, hot California climate (which mostly produces quick-maturing wines), and fertile California soil, raise eyebrows and doubts about the state's abundant yields and showy fruit. And while it is true that there is more similarity between one Napa vintage and another than there is between different years in the time-honored wine regions

1994 NAPA VALLEY VINTAGE AT A GLANCE

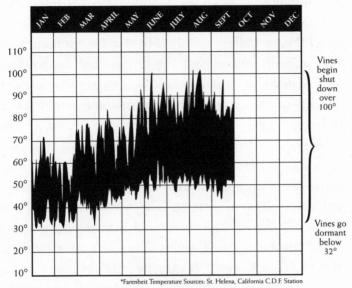

| | JAN | FEB | MAR | APRIL | MAY | JUNE | JULY | AUG | SEPT | OCT | NOV | DEC |

110°
100°   Vines
90°   begin
80°   shut
70°   down
60°   over
50°   100°
40°
30°   Vines go
20°   dormant
10°   below
            32°

*Farenheit Temperature Sources: St. Helena, California C.D.F. Station

57

GROWING SEASON

		BUD	BLOOM	VÉRAISON	HARVEST			Growing Days
Sauvignon Blanc								194
Chardonnay								197+
Pinot Noir								177
Cabernet Sauvignon								

Total Growing Season

RAINFALL

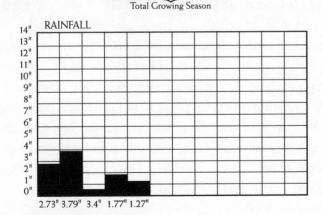

14"
13"
12"
11"
10"
9"
8"
7"
6"
5"
4"
3"
2"
1"
0"

2.73" 3.79" 3.4" 1.77" 1.27"

Source: The Napa Valley Vintner's Association
This chart is an example of the type of tool used to analyze a vintage. It is a snapshot synopsis of the climatic season.

of Europe, we can look to other up-and-coming, cool-climate wine regions for climatic and qualitative variety.

California is not just Napa anymore. I don't mean to knock Napa Valley, which is by far the Golden State's most famous region and the undisputed champion of American wines; still, even in Napa things are changing. Having been reproached for producing wines too fat and ripe to be true, the Napa natives are taking their vineyards onto the cooler hillsides—as do their European mentors—nestling them in wooded slopes above the valley floor. There the air is cooler and the soil more barren, forcing the vines to "suffer" and develop character. More varietal plantings can also be found these days in Carneros, in the cooler, southern part of Napa County. It may be that the vines in such new climate and soil areas need more time to mature before their wines can be judged. Still, Napa vintners are adding an even larger spectrum of variety and complexity to their wines.

So what happened in 1994, and which wines are worth cellaring? Perhaps the only common denominator shared by California wine regions in 1994 was their late-starting and long-lasting harvests, which made for balanced, healthy, and flavorful fruit. The red varieties steal the show, since they most benefited from the cooler, longer growing season, and were the least affected by late-season rainfalls. The whites did not fare as well, save for those in southern counties, where the late-October harvests produced intense, complex, and tropical-fruit-flavored grapes. The year as a whole provided some excellent prime materials, and promises ageable, tightly structured wines.

In general, California saw cool weather throughout the spring and summer of 1994, with temperatures ranging from 75 to 85 degrees F in the daytime, and falling to around 50 at night. This cooler weather brought the tonnage, or yields, down; brought the acids levels up; and extended the growing season, allowing good maturity with no raising or overripening. The reds of 1994 should thus prove to be concentrated, with aging potential.

Mendocino County, in northern California, is generally warmer than northern Sonoma (except for its Anderson Valley, which has fog and coastal breezes due to its proximity to the ocean). Its 1994 crops were down a bit. A cool, dry winter was followed by a warm but not excessively hot summer and a very dry fall—barring one storm in early October, which brought little actual precipitation. The region's 1994 Zinfandels might be worth cellaring.

Sonoma has promising Pinot Noirs. The ocean-cooled areas of the Russian River Valley, Alexander Valley, and Dry Creek Valley, with their deep, loose, well-drained loam soils, have conditions best suited for the Pinot Noir. And 1994's harvest weather only aided this inherent tendency. A cool summer, warm August, and very cool September provided a very long growing season. The only storm, near October 3, might have had ill effects on some Chardonnays and Sauvignon Blancs. Zinfandel and Gewurztraminer production were down as well. The good news is that the Pinot Noir thrives under such harvest conditions, as does the Merlot, and wines of these two varieties may well prove to have a superlative vintage.

Napa, whose most famous grape is the Cabernet Sauvignon, is counting on 1994 as a top vintage. The long, cool growing season, with no heat spurts, no rain, and lots of hang time, made for grapes and wines with great flavors. The only blip in an otherwise picture-perfect season was a hot spell during the first two weeks in August, which caused uneven *véraison*. But by thinning out the poorly colored fruits, growers allowed their vines to concentrate on the remaining grapes. With some harvests lasting well into November, there is a lot of potential for balanced wines. That long, cool growing season was also ideal for tannin and color development. The wines of 1994 should thus be softer and more acceptable at first release, yet still have the long-range pH and acid balance necessary for proper aging. Count on exceptional red wine varieties from 1994, with Napa's hallmark Cabernets in first place; among the whites there will also be fresh and spicy Sauvignon Blancs and complex, steely Chardonnays.

The Sierra Foothill counties such as Amador and Eldorado were making premium wines back during the 1880s and 1890s, when frustrated gold seekers turned to grape growing. Some say that the only reason this region fell by the wayside, so to speak, was its transportation problems; there is no "Napa River" in the foothills, and the mountains made it almost impossible for the original winemakers to get their wares to market.

The Zinfandels grown here, especially in Amador's Shenandoah Valley, have high sugar, high acidity, and an intensity of flavor not found elsewhere in the state. Some ascribe this to the warm days, cool nights, and volcanic soil; others to the nonirrigated, low-yield, ancient vineyards. The cool, wet spring and Indian summer of 1994 brought tonnage down about 20 to 30 percent, but also created much concentration of flavor—a year worth cellaring.

It has been said that the visitor who travels south instead of north from San Francisco may get a clearer concept of the past, present, and future of premium California wines. Assuming that south of San Francisco, California gets progressively warmer, many imagine the wines become heavier and flabbier than those farther up the coast. What most don't realize, however, is that the valleys of California's Central Coast—as opposed to the Central Valley—are cooler in the summer than much of the state farther north; latitude plays a larger role than longitude, because the valley heat draws in the cool ocean breezes.

The growing season of 1994 saw a wide range of results due to heavy rains. Luckily, the rains that came just as picking was to begin were followed by cool winds that kept the grapes dry and in good health. As with the rest of the state, the unusually cool summer delayed the beginning of harvest by almost a month, and the smaller yields are promising very concentrated fruits.

Monterey, Santa Clara, and Santa Cruz . . . It was here that the Franciscan monks first planted grapes in 1777, and that the great names of the early California wine industry chose to make their home. After being nearly eaten up by urban development, this historic wine region is making a comeback via younger winemakers, who have set up camp in the San Benito Mountains, the Salinas Valley, and the Santa Cruz Mountains.

Monterey's grapevines tend to produce buds two weeks earlier than other regions, and the fall harvest typically begins two weeks later than in other regions, providing a full extra month of hang time. The harvest in 1994 started even later than usual. The first grapes were picked in mid-September, with the last grapes harvested in late November. The year produced good Chardonnays, Pinot Noirs, and Merlots. Because of lower yields and good acids, the wines are proving long on richness and elegance.

The heart of the Central Coast—a region that includes Paso Robles, Edna Valley, and Arroyo Grande Valley—is one of California's best-kept secrets. It is an extremely variable region; the temperature ranges from warm (inland) to very cool (coast), the soil from loamy sands to calcareous shales. Unfortunately, harvesting was problematic in 1994

61

due to heavy, late-September rains. However, the Pinot Noirs seemed to do well here that year.

It is no surprise that Santa Barbara County, primarily comprised of the Santa Maria and Santa Ynez Valleys, is quickly becoming the viticultural heart of California. The effect of the ocean is at its most dramatic here, because the coastline makes a sudden right-angle turn, and the mountains change direction as well. The resulting two valleys cradle the only mountain range in North America that runs east-west, not north-south, and hence lie directly exposed to the Pacific. It is here that some of the state's greatest Chardonnays and Pinot Noirs are produced, and 1994 will confirm that.

Overall, California's 1994 vintage was very "French," if I may dare to say so. The magic combination was the long, cool growing season; the lower yields; and the dearth of rain at the right time. The resulting "never-ending" harvest extracted the excellent, forthright fruits that California wines are famous for, yet in a tame fashion. Because there was not too much heat, there should not be many heavy, overly alcoholic, "madeirized" wines around; and while the lack of needed acids is often a problem in California, 1994's wines have them. The year's wines are balanced, with good potential for maturation; they are good candidates for your collection.

Analyzing a Vintage: Burgundy 1993

The 1993 Burgundy harvest has turned out to surpass all initial assessments and is definitely worth collecting—if you can still get your hands on some! After two rather average years, the 1993 harvest proved to be the best since the 1989 and 1990; it is rivaled (and perhaps succeeded) only by the 1995. In early September 1993, winemakers were counting on a great success, but Mother Nature had planned things differently: The rest of the month was marked by heavy precipitation. Still, the key words for the year were *low yields* and *savoir faire,* and the better winemakers offered some very concentrated wines.

The weather in Burgundy has always been variable; that is part of the region's charm, and one of the main reasons that it produces some of the world's very best wines. All red Burgundy wines are issued from the Pinot Noir grape, and all whites from the Chardonnay. Both varieties often struggle to reach full ripeness, but this apparent flaw is actually a source of elegance and quality in the resulting wines. Moreover, the climate differs greatly between Dijon and Mâcon on any given day, and the soil varies from vineyard to vineyard—even from step to step. It is this unique trinity of climate, grape, and soil that makes the magic happen.

Beau jour de l'An, beau mois d'août. This old Burgundian adage claims that if New Year's Day is sunny and warm, so will be the month of August—which is exactly what happened in 1993. The winter pruning, as you now know, is the first task of the year, and never starts before January 22; it is the factor determining the yield of the next vintage. In 1993, it got under way in a mild climate. The following months made for a winter sufficiently cool and humid.

April announced the start of spring with high temperatures and the first rainstorms. Despite rather heavy hail, particularly in Chablis and Mâcon, the heat favored a rapid start to vegetation growth. By mid-April—between the 15th and the 20th—budding out was complete in all vineyards and for all grape varieties.

The perturbations continued throughout May and June, bringing on the first signs of mildew. Temperatures

63

remained higher than normal, and the hail returned to several parts of the Côte d'Or. Yet this agitation did not stop the rapid evolution of the vegetation; in fact, it led to an early and homogenous flowering. Repeated fluctuations between warm and cold temperatures allowed a regrouping of the flowering, starting on the first days of June and peaking around June 8 and 9. This meant a complete flowering in less than fifteen days, evenly, from Chablis to Mâcon.

The summer climate was practically ideal—warm and dry so as to permit a good *véraison* as well as the enrichment of sugars. The sunny, hot days and fresh evenings of August stopped any development of gray rot (which was a very real risk considering the high mildew levels brought on by the rains) and greatly accelerated maturation.

The beginning of September raised hopes for an outstanding and balanced vintage. The maturation conditions were good; acid and anthocyanin levels were up; and sugar levels were, in some cases, higher than in previous years. In fact, 1993 was the sixth consecutive year of an early maturation. Then came the late rains, between the 7th and 14th and the 20th and 24th of September. The first one happily unblocked a maturation that had been stalled, paradoxically, by the lack of rain since mid-July, and caused a small increase in grape weight without having very much influence on the harvest volumes. The second rain, however, slowed the maturation again and resulted in a slight decrease in sugar levels.

What is considered a determinant of the 1993 vintage's quality is the period in which the winemaker chose to harvest the grapes. A majority of the harvests were accomplished under sunny skies, but it is very important to know whether they occurred before or after the second rain. It is true that the Pinot Noir, in most cases, was free of disease and very healthy. The fresh temperatures that accompanied the late rain impeded the onset of botrytis (which can be detrimental to the color extraction of red wine) and helped increase the wine's aromatic potential. Still, it has some structural problems due to a lack of concentration.

As for the more fragile Chardonnay, this same freshness brought on widespread attacks of gray rot toward the end of the harvest. The whites were far more affected by the rain, especially those situated on hilltops, because they were so exposed.

As one winemaker from Beaune explained, "As far as the reds are concerned, the grapes harvested before the second rains had a good maturity level and made very good wines. Otherwise, those who waited, brought in a very soggy harvest and will have wines with less color. . . . It got a little panicky near the end because the rain made it almost impossible for the tractors to work the vines. We even had to drain the grapes; they were 60 to 80 percent water."

The white wines of 1993 are inferior to 1992's and, allowing for a few exceptions, are diluted and lacking in body. They very much suffered from the rain, especially in Chablis and Mâcon (St.-Véran excluded!). The reds clearly survived better and are colorful and aromatic.

Now we can, and should, break down Burgundy by region and examine the different appellations and their microclimates, so that you may better understand how you can judge a vintage yourself.

Chablis

The seventy-nine hundred acres of Chablis (thirty years ago there were only fifteen hundred) got more than their

65

fair share of storms in 1993. Despite this, a rapid and premature flowering occurred under excellent conditions. The harvest started under sunny skies around September 20 (considered very early) but finished under heavy rain and with signs of oncoming gray rot. There were also some cases of overproduction, not necessarily the fault of the winemakers. And, as you know, large yields coupled with rain lead to even greater dilution. This means a Chardonnay with lower alcohol levels—up to 1 percent lower in some vineyards—putting the whites at about 10.5 percent vol. before chaptalization. It also means higher levels of acidity, which creates wines a little less rich or fat than 1992's, but also more vigorous and fresh—very much in the style of a true Chablis.

Côte d'Or

The "golden slope" comprised of the Côte de Nuits and the Côte de Beaune is only thirty miles long and a half mile wide, yet it is home to the several hundred premiers and grands crus largely responsible for Burgundy's legendary reputation. For the most part the harvests in the Côte de Nuits began around September 20, just before the second rain, and in some areas continued until the end of the month. Considering that this region's wines were heavily affected by the second rain and, therefore, slightly less concentrated, the Pinot Noir is a success, with surprise results from Marsannay and—of course— the classic contender, Vosne-Romanée.

The Pinot Noirs that defied the negative influences of the downpours are firm and solid, with an intense black cherry color, and big, powerful aromas. When it comes to this vintage, said a winemaker in Gevrey-Chambertin, "People are going to be speaking of elegance and allure, but not in terms of typicity and not by simply comparing it to another vintage because of its style or personality. Nineteen ninety-three makes me think of 1988 or 1990, not because of its taste, but because of its great race."

The Côte de Beaune's Pinot Noirs also deserve rave reviews. This was the least affected region of the Côte d'Or; the harvest started around either the 18th or the 27th, in both cases avoiding the rains. And as one wine-maker in Pommard explained, "The rains had only an external effect; the water didn't really have time to enter into the plant by the roots. That's not to say, though, that we didn't have a harvest that was a little soggy. There was a phenomenon of dilution. We lost about 3 percent to 4 percent of sugar concentration, putting the level of alco-hol at 12.2 percent instead of 12.5 percent volume."

The reds are likely to be concentrated enough but might lack for tannin, which could mean a very supple and elegant wine or, again, a diluted, unbalanced one. There are interesting 1993 wines from Savigny-Les-Beaune, Pommard, Volnay, Auxey-Duresses, and Sante-nay, where the grapes came in healthy, deeply colored, and fully matured.

Côte Chalonnaise and Mâconnais

Mâcon produces 36 percent of Burgundy's white wines, because it is here that the classic acidity of the Chardon-nay grape is soothed and placated by the less calcareous soil. Red Mâconnais are issued from Gamay grapes, as in Beaujolais, but here, too, the soil gives them a different style than their neighbor's.

Like Chablis, this region was hard hit by hailstorms throughout 1993. Again, those grapes brought in before

September 22 (Mâcon received up to thirty-two inches of rain on that day) were healthy and relatively mature with reasonable yields. Afterward, the less ripe grapes stalled in maturation, and gray rot began to set in.

The whites will be lacking in body but not without the presence of aromas such as grapefruit, honey, and almonds. The reds will be less intense in color and concentration but surprisingly robust. Wines from Mercurey, Rully, and Givry are likely to offer a good quality:price ratio in 1993. The best bets in Mâcon are from St.-Véran.

Beaujolais

Beaujolais escaped the deluges of 1993, because most winemakers harvested as early as the 12th or, in some cases, the 8th of September. The Gamay wines are colorful and rich, and flavored with strawberries, spices, plums, cherries, and chocolate. There is talk of a resemblance to the 1991 vintage, which would mean that the best crus should last as long as ten years, instead of the usual three to five. The 1993 Beaujolais promises a more homogenous quality. The wines have lots of fruit and tannin, and an acidity level a little higher than normal. They are balanced and truly convey the typical fruitiness of Beaujolais.

If it's true what they say about only one year in three being a good vintage in Burgundy, because of the erratic weather conditions, then of the trio 1991 through 1993, that year is 1993. Despite the strange paradox of September's heat-induced stalled maturations and late rains, the headstrong and unpredictable Pinot Noir reigned. Although you can expect inconsistent quality from region to region (the bane of Burgundy!), remember that this same fault is also

Burgundy's strongest attribute and a major facet of its wine's personality.

Two examples of harvest reports: two different vintages, two different countries. Although it is true that the average wine collector is not going to go through all of this work and research, the information is available to you if you wish to study a particular region in more depth. You don't need a degree in agronomy, or in chemistry. It comes down to just common sense and logic. If you have developed your personal taste and preferences, use vintage charts as initial guides, and then look a little further; you can rely upon your own opinion to establish your collection.

69

CHAPTER 3

FORMING THE COLLECTION

"One barrel of wine can work more miracles than a church full of saints."

—Italian proverb

This chapter is going to take you step by step through the decision-making process of building your wine collection. You probably have a good idea of what you like, what you want, what you can afford, and how to get it. It is now time to create a collection suited to your needs and tastes.

WHICH WINES SHOULD BE CELLARED, AND FOR HOW LONG?

Now that you know how a wine is made, the importance of climate during the growing season, and how and why a wine ages, identifying which wines merit cellaring and for how long should be much easier. The guidelines are simple, because personal taste plays a large role in deciding when a wine is best to drink. Remember that the "top" vintages—those providing all of the right climatic conditions—are those that best guarantee aging capacity in a wine. Remember also that two bottles of the same wine from the same château but from different vintages can have different aging potentials.

So which wines will have a longer life? Moving from the general to the specific, choose a red wine over a dry white wine, except for some of the great dry Burgundies and sweet white wines; a wine from a cold climate rather than a hot (with the latter's shorter growing season); and a wine issued from a noble grape variety rather than a lighter one (a Pinot Noir over a Chinon, for example).

Wines to Drink

Wines meant to be drunk rapidly—within a year of their vintage—are those that are fruity and simple. These include most ordinary, inexpensive red and white wines; all *vins de table*; all wines called "nouveau," such as Beaujolais Nouveau; "village" wines; rosé and *gris* wines; and most inexpensive white German, Alsatian, Loire Valley, and New World white wines. A generic Bordeaux, Chianti, or Cabernet Sauvignon might even fit into this category; don't make the mistake of assuming that a Cabernet Sauvignon is automatically to be laid down. Consider the region's climate and the vintage, and ask yourself if enough tannins and alcohol are present to carry the fruit through for a couple of years.

AUSTRALIA
Sémillon-Sauvignon, Cape Mentelle, Margaret River
Sauvignon Blanc, Shaw 1 Smith, Adelaide Hills
Chardonnay, Pipers Brook, Tasmania
Chardonnay, McLaren Vale, Seaview
Merlot, South Eastern Australia Nottage Hill, Hardy's

CHILE
Chardonnay, Aconcagua Casablanca Vineyard, Villard

Chardonnay, Central Valley, Bel Arbor
Sauvignon Blanc, Curico District, Echeverria
Merlot, Maipo Valley Santa Maria Vineyard, Alameda

FRANCE
Pinot Blanc Martin Lahr, Cave Coopérative de Ribeauvillé,
    Alsace
Claude Thomas, Sancerre à Chavignol, Loire
Vigne Blanche, Henri Bourgeois, Sancerre
Domaine La Grave Chardonnay, Minervois
Domaine du Grand Mayne, white, Côtes de Duras
Domaine Grand Veneur, Viognier, Côtes-du-Rhône
Domaine de Mas Crémat, Côtes du Roussillon

ITALY
Soave Classico Sanvincenzo, Anselmi, Veneto
Chardonnay, Castello della Sala, Antinori
Pinot Grigio Aquileia del Friuli, Castello D'Albola, northeast
    Italy
Pinot Grigio Fontana Candida, northeast Italy
Orvieto Classico Secco Vigneto Torricella, BIGI, Umbria
Chianti, Straccali, Tuscany
Chianti Colli Senesi Titolato Colombaia, Riccardo Falchini,
    Tuscany

PORTUGAL
Chardonnay, Casa Santos Lima, Quinta do Boavista,
    Alenquer
Casa de Sezim, Vinho Verde, Guimaraes
Quinta do Tamariz, Vinho Verde, Carreira
Requengos VQPD Vinho Blanco
Cartuxa Evora VQPRD, vinho blanco
Quinta do Carmo, Vin de Pays, vinho blanco
Alentejo Vinho Regional CR & F

USA

Chardonnay Willamette Valley Barrel Fermented, Duck Pond, Oregon

Chenin Blanc, Dry Creek Vineyard

White Zinfandel, Sutter Home

Semillon, Clos du Val, Napa

Riesling Dry Oregon Reserve, Van Duzer, Oregon

Riesling Late Harvest, Yakima Valley, Covey Run, Washington

Fumé Blanc, Columbia Valley, Hogue, Washington

Sauvignon Blanc, Lake County Buena Vista, Mendocino

Johanisberg Riesling, Columbia Valley, Snoqualmie, Washington

Wines for One to Three Years (Short-Term Wines)

These are delicate wines, because you must open them while they still have their fruits yet right before they turn. This is a larger category than you would think: It encompasses most wines on the market. They are higher in quality than the "Wines to Drink" and include the German Qualitätsweins; a petit Chablis (rather than a grand cru Chablis); varieties such as Chardonnay (except for grand cru Burgundies); Chenin Blancs; Sauvignon Blancs; most Italian whites and reds; the Côtes du Rhône-Villages; most wines from the middle and south of France, such as Languedoc-Roussillon and Provence; the less important Bordeaux and Burgundies; and most of the Loire Valley wines. Champagnes should also be placed in this category, because they do not mature with age.

AUSTRALIA

Chardonnay Victoria, Milburn Park

Cabernet Sauvignon Western Australia Wildflower Ridge, Houghton

Shiraz Longhorne Creek, Bleasdale

73

CHILE
Chardonnay, Concha y Toro
Chardonnay Maule Proprietor s Reserve, Carta Vieja
Merlot Rapel Reserve, Carmen
Cabernet Sauvignon Curico, Montes
Cabernet Sauvignon Curico, Valley El Descanso Estate,
    Errazuriz
Cabernet Sauvignon Valle del Cachapoal, Vina Porta

FRANCE
Tokay Pinot Gris, Dopff au Moulin, Riquewihr, Alsace
Riesling Haguenau, Cave Coopérative de Ribeauvillé, Alsace
Pierre Jacques Druet, Bourgeuil, Loire
Peyres Nobles, red, Corbières
Cuvée Mathilde, Château Canos, Corbières
Château Romasson, Domaines Ott, Bandol, Provence
Château du Galoupet, red, Provence
Le Crédo, VDP Pays de Catalans, Cazes Frères, Roussillon
Domaine Lerys, Fitou, Languedoc
Clos Triguedina, Baldes et Fils, Cahors, Lot
La Tour Boisée, Minervois
Domaine du Vieux Bourg, red, Côtes de Duras
La Tour Boisée, Minervois
Château de Beaucastel, Châteauneuf-du-Pape, Côte du Rhône
Rully "Les Cailloux," Vignoble Sounit, Rully, Burgundy
Château de Chamirey, Antonin Rodet, Burgundy
Château Haut Bertinerie, Côtes de Bordeaux
Château Pape-Clément, white, Bordeaux

ITALY
Chardonnay, Trentino i Mesi, Casa Girelli, northeast
Tocai Friulano Grave del Friuli, Borgo Magredo, northeast
Sangiovese Conti Contini, Capezzana, Tuscany
Solane Valpolicella Classico, Santi, Veneto

74

Chianti Classico, Castello di Verrazzano, Tuscany
Barbera d Asti, Cascina la Barbatella, Piedmont
Montepulciano d Abruzzo, Farnese
Dolcetto d'Alba Augenta, Pelissero, Piedmont

PORTUGAL
Douro Charamba, Avelada
Garrafeira, Casa Agricola Herdeiros de D. Luis de Margaride,
    Ribatejo
Trincadeira, Herdade do Esorao, Lisbon
Reguengos, Vinho Tinto, Adega Cooperativa de Reguengos

SPAIN
Rioja Faustino VII, Bodegas Faustino Martinez
Valdemar Tinto, Martinez Bujunda, Rioja
Conde de Valdemar Ciranza, Martinez Bujunda, Rioja

75

UNITED STATES
Chardonnay, Herman Wente Vineyard, Napa
Chardonnay, Calera, San Benito
Chardonnay, Gallo, North Sonoma
Chardonnay, Robert Mondavi, Napa
Gewurztraminer Rogue Valley, Foris, Oregon
Merlot, Clos du Bois, Napa
Merlot, Kendall Jackson Vintner's Reserve, Sonoma
Zinfandel Amador County Pokerville, Karly, Sierra Foothills

Wines for Three to Seven Years (Medium-Term Wines)

This category is where things start getting interesting, and
wines from it will probably make up the larger part of your
cellar. Five years is a good apogee year for lighter wines, as
well as for average vintages of quality wines; it is also a
good year in which to start drinking heavier wines, which,

although young, are fruity and charming at this stage. Wines in this category are well structured, balanced, full bodied, and take on personality and complexity after several years of aging. They include Bordeaux's crus bourgeois, as well as the equivalent from other regions; lighter vintages from Burgundy, such as Chambolle, Rully, Savigny, Volnay, and Beaune; lighter vintages of Cahors, Buzet, and Madiran; most red California and Australian wines; Reserva Chiantis; Chilean wines; and all quality whites, except for some dry Bordeaux and all of the sweet wines (German, Sauternes, Jura, and so on).

AUSTRALIA
Chardonnay Hunter Valley Roxburgh, Rosemount
Pinot Noir, Coldstream Hills Reserve, Yarra Valley
Cabernet Sauvignon, Wynns Coonawarra Estate, Coonawarra

CHILE
Cabernet Sauvignon Maipo Valley Private Reserve, Canepa
Cabernet Sauvignon Colchagua, Casa Lapostolle

FRANCE
Tokay Pinot Gris Reserve, Dopff au Moulin, Alsace
Riesling Steinacker, Cave Coopérative de Ribeauvillé, Alsace
Gewurztraminer Pflänzer, Cave Coopérative de Ribeauvillé, Alsace
Château de Chenonceau, Loire
Bourgueil chez Nau, Loire
Paul Gaudinot's St. Nicolas de Bourgueil, Loire
Savennières, Le Clos du Papillon, Domaine du Closel, Loire
Château de Villeneuve, Jean-Pierre Chevallier, Saumur-Champigny, Loire
Domaine de la Moussière, Alphonse Mellot, Sancerre
Château du Pibarnon, Provence

Château Simone, Provence
Château Coussin, Cuvée César, Châteaux Elie Sumeire,
    Provence
Domaine de Rimauresq, Côtes de Provence
Mas du Soleilla, Corbières
Château de Mont-Redon, Châteauneuf-du-Pape, Côtes du
    Rhône
Gilles Barge, Ampuis, Condrieu
Marsannay Domaine Collotte, Burgundy
Château de Rully, Antonin Rodet, Burgundy
Chablis Grand Cru "Les Preuses," René et Vincent Dauvissat,
    Burgundy
Nuits St. Georges 1er Cru, Maison Moillard-Grivot, Burgundy
Château Pape-Clément, Bordeaux
Château La Tour Guillotin, Puisseguin St. Emilion, Bordeaux

GERMANY
Erdener Treppchen Riesling Spätlese, Alfred Merkelbach,
    Mosel
Feilbingerter Konigsgarten Riesling Trockenbeerenauslese,
    Adolf Lotzbeyer, Nahe
Ruppertsburger Reiterpfad Riesling Auslese, J.F. Kimich,
    Rheinpfalz

ITALY
Villa Bianchi Verdicchio dei Castelli di Jesi Classico Superiore,
    Umani Ronchi
Falerno del Massico D.O.C. Bianco Classico, Villa Matilde,
    Compania
Chianti Colli Fiorentini Il Cortile, Castello Guicciardini,
    Tuscany
Chianti Colli Fiorentini Il Cortile, Castello Guicciardini,
    Tuscany
Chianti Classico Riserva, Castello di Verrazzano, Tuscany

Cancelli, Badia A Coltibuono, Tuscany
Valpolicella Classico Superiore Villa Rizzardi Poiega,
    Guerrieri-rizzardi, Veneto
Montepulciano d'Abruzzo, Masciarelli

PORTUGAL
Douro Foral Garrafeira, Caves Alianca
Dao Duque de Viseu, Sogrape
Dao, Caves Velhas
Mouchao Tinto, Herdade do Mouchao, Casa Branca, Sousel
Quinta da Gaivosa, Domingos Alves de Sousa, Douro
Quinta de Saes, Alvaro Manuel Albuquerque Figeiredo e
    Castro, Dao
Quinta do Cotto, Grande Escolha, Douro
Cabernet Sauvignon, Quinta da Bacalhoa, Azeitao

SPAIN
Fronsola Gran Vina sol (white), Torrès, Pénedes
Muffato della Sala (white) Antinori
Magdala Pinot Noir
Rioja Don Jacobo Crianza, Bodegas Corral
Rioja Vina Real Crianza, Cune

UNITED STATES
Chardonnay, Cuvaison Reserve, California
Pinot Noir, Byron, California
Jensen Pinot Noir, Mt. Harlan AVA, Calera,California
Merlot, Leonetti, Washington
Bonny Doon "le Cigare Volant," California
Bonny Doon Ca'del Solo, Il Fiasco, California
Cabernet Sauvignon, Wente Charles Wetmore Vineyard,
    California
Cabernet Sauvignon, La Jota California
Cabernet Sauvignon, Freemark Abbey California

Cabernet Sauvignon, Beaulieu California

Cabernet Sauvignon, Kendall Jackson, Gold Coast Vineyards, California

Cabernet Sauvignon, Palmer Vineyards, Long Island, New York

Wines for Seven Years and More (Long-Term Wines)

The wines in this category are those red wines that have high tannin levels and need a minimum of ten years: the grands crus of Bordeaux and Burgundy; the best Côtes du Rhônes (Hermitage); Piedmont's Barolos and Barbarescos; Tuscany's Brunellos; Spain's Rioja Reservas; as well as the best California and Australian Cabernets. Great white Burgundies, Bordeaux, and all of the great sweet wines also need at least ten years.

These wines need the most careful monitoring and follow-up. For example, if you have a white Burgundy—a Meursault—that has an estimated maturation date of ten to fifteen years, open your test case and start sampling in the fifth or sixth year. This way, you don't waste bottles by unnecessarily opening them early, and you can judge for yourself when they become enjoyable to drink. Don't think, either, that you have to wait until the "perfect" moment. Learn to enjoy the wines at different stages of development. If you do find that you have waited too long—the wine is at what you would consider its peak, and you have six cases of it—don't panic. Generally, a wine will stay at its peak approximately the same number of years that it took to reach its peak. Again, the variables in this equation are your personal taste, the vintage, and the wine.

It is a little more difficult to decide how many of these wines you need to stock. Obviously, the goal is to buy the wines young, when they're less expensive, and drink them when they've doubled their price! Remember also that the longer the wine needs to age, the more bottles you will need, because you are going to have to test it more often. You want to avoid the problem of having no bottles left to drink.

AUSTRALIA
Yarra Yering Dry Red No. 1
Shiraz, Barossa Old Block, St. Hallett
Shiraz, South Australia Grange, Penfolds
Shiraz, Henschke Hill of Grace
Cabernet Sauvignon, Keyneton Cyril, Henschke
Cabernet Sauvignon, Penfold's Bin 707
Cabernet Sauvignon, Parker Estate Terra Rossa First Growth
Grange Hermitage, Penfolds

CHILE
Cabernet Sauvignon, Maipo Puente Alto, Vineyard Don
    Melchor Private Reserve, Concha y Toro
Cabernet Sauvignon, Los Vascos Reserva

FRANCE
Beyer Gewurztraminer SGN, Alsace
Hugel Tokay VT, Alsace
Riesling Osterberg Grand Cru, Cave Coopérative de
    Ribeauvillé, Alsace
Tokay Sélection de Grains Nobles, Domaine Weinbach of
    Colette Faller
Château du Hureau - Philippe Vatan, Saumur-Champigny, Loire
Château de Fesles, Bonnezeaux, Loire
Domaine de la Cour d Ardenay, Coteaux du Layon, Loire
Etienne Guigal S.A., Côte Rôtie
Yves Cuilleron, Chavanay, Condrieu, Côte Rôtie
Côtes du Juras "vin jaune" Château d'Arlay, Compte de la
    Guiche

Chablis Premier Cru "Bougros," La Chablisienne, Chablis
Chambolle Musigny, Domaine Jacques-Frédéric Mugnier,
    Burgundy
Vosne Romanée 1er Cru "Les Suchots," Louis Latour, Burgundy
Chambolle Musigny, Maison Moillard Grivot, Burgundy
Echezeaux Grand Cru, Mongeard-Mugneret, Burgundy
Pommard-Épenots 1er Cru, Domaine Mussy, Burgundy
Richebourg, Gros, Burgundy
Clos Vougeot, Domaine Amiot-Servelle, Chambolle-Musigny,
    Burgundy
Comté Armand, Clos des Épeneaux, Pommard, Burgundy
Vosne Romanée "Aux Réas" Gerbet, Burgundy
Château La Conseillante, Pomerol
Château de France, Graves
Château Smith-Haut-Lafitte, Graves
Château Chasse-Spleen, Médoc
Château Cantenac-Brown, Margaux
Château Lynch-Bages, Pauillac
Château Pichon-Longueville, Comtesse de Lalande, Pauillac
Château Les Ormes-de-Pez, St. Estephe
Château Branaire-Ducru, St.-Julien
Château Léoville-Barton, St.-Julien

81

GERMANY
Müller-Catoir, Riesling, Pfalz
Kurt Darting, Rheinpfalz
Brauneberger Juffer-Sonnenuhr, Fritz Haag, Mosel-Saar-Ruwer
Abtsberg, C. von Schubert, Maximin Grünhaus, Mosel-Saar-
    Ruwer
Egon Müller, Saar
Heyl zu Herrnsheim, Mosel

ITALY
Barbaresco Riserva, Borgogno

Barolo Riserva Especiale, Terre del Barolo
La Vigna di Sonvico, Cascina La Barbatella
Brunello di Montalcino, Lisini S. Angelo in Colle
Sammarco, Castello di Rampolla
Turriga, Argiolas
Recioto di Soave "Dei Capitelli" (sweet white), Anselmi,
    Veneto
Sassicaia, Tenuta San Guido (Marchesi Incisa della Rocchetta),
    Tuscany

PORTUGAL
Moscatel de Setubal, José Maria do Fonseca, Azeitao
Periquita, Terras do Sado, José Maria do Donseca, Azeitao
Quinta do Carmo
Ferreira Barca Velha
J.M. Fonseca Tinto Velho Rosado Fernandes

SPAIN
Penedès Gran Coronas "Mas la Plana" Reserva, Torrès
Marquès de Caceres Gran Reserva
Marquès de Riscal Riserva, Rioja
Gran Coronas Mas Rabell de Fontenac, Torrès
Ribera del Duero, Vega Sicilia "Unico"
Cosme Palacio y Hermanos, Cosecha, Bodegas Palacio, Rioja
Martinez Bujanda Reserva, Rioja
Pesquera Ribero del Duero
Marqués de Murrieta Castillo de Ygay Gran Reserva

UNITED STATES
Syrah, Bien Nacido Vineyard, Qupé
Pinot Noir, Willamette Valley Reserve, Ponzi, Oregon
Cabernet Sauvignon, Caymus, Napa
Cabernet Sauvignon Reserve, Clos du Val, Napa
Cabernet Sauvignon, Château St. Jean, Sonoma

Cabernet Sauvignon, Far Niente
Cabernet/Merlot, Hedges Red Mountain Reserve
Cabernet Sauvignon Reserve, Beaulieu Vineyards, Napa
Niebaum Coppola, F.F. Coppola, Napa
Opus One, Mondavi/Rothschild, Napa

The list above is by no means an exhaustive or defini-
tive qualitative choice. It is meant to be a rough guide to
better help you categorize your own selections. There are
so many wines I would have liked to include but could not
because of lack of space, and because that is not the object
of the exercise. You may feel that some of the wines are in
the wrong age-potential category, or that some countries
are better represented than others. First of all, drinking the
wines when you find them the most attractive is more
important than categorizing these; second, I very well may
have made mistakes in my judgments of certain regions
with which I am not familiar enough; and third, wine aging
potentials can really vary between appellations, regions,
winemakers, and vintages, as we have determined, so it is
impossible, and defeatist, to try to impose rigid parameters.

There are also many other countries that have been
omitted or only touched upon. In the "drink now" and
"short-term" categories, for example, I could have listed
far more German and Spanish wines, but I personally find
that wines from those categories in those countries not
always worth drinking, and so did not include them until
the "medium," or "long-term" category.

Please don't forget the wonderful wines in countries
that were not included. No cellar would be complete
without a bottle of Lebanon s Château Musar, Etchart's
Malbec from Argentina, a Cloudy Bay New Zealand
Sauvignon Blanc, Greece's Château Carras, or a Hungarian Tokaji.

83

HOW MUCH TO BUY?

When buying the wine for your collection, you need to know which quantities to purchase, and in which proportions. Generally, it is a good idea to buy only as much of the first category—"Wines to Drink"—as you would drink in three months. From the last category, "Long-Term Wines," you should buy as much as you can, or as much as you can afford. Also, as noted earlier, the longer the wine will be cellared, the more of it you will need, because you will test it as it evolves. For example, if you buy six bottles of a wine that will be ready to drink in about ten years and open one at the time of purchase, one three years later, another in the fifth year, and a fourth in the eighth year—you'll only have two bottles left in the tenth year, when the wine is at its best!

The following formulas are classic for collecting your red and white wine stocks. The first was refined by Hugh Johnson, and you may need to alter it according to your preferences. It is a good starting point. Afterward, I will give you several sample cellars with generic regional guidelines, so that all you need do is plug in a wine from the previous lists, or choose your own.

Formula #1

(The number of bottles of a particular wine that you would like to drink in a year) × (the number of years it needs to mature) = your stock

If you drink, say, 1 bottle a week of a Bordeaux Supérieur, this formula translates into 52 bottles per year × 5 years = 260 bottles. The number of bottles you will need to buy annually to replace those you open is the

same as your annual consumption figure, or, in this case,
52 bottles.

Wines to Drink:

You may assume that there is no point in stocking wines that
are meant to drink immediately, since you can buy them as
needed. But even having a case of wine from this category
on hand will save you time, trouble, and money. If you think
about it, any wine from any of these categories is available
for immediate purchase. Nothing can stop you from going
out and buying a twenty-year-old bottle of Bordeaux—but,
again, you'll pay top dollar and run the risks associated with
not knowing its storage and transport history.

White wines. Your maximum stock will equal the number
of bottles drunk in three months. I drink an average of
four bottles of wine a week, excluding parties or dinners.
Usually, two of them are red and two white; of these two
whites, one is generally a young wine and the other a
more expensive, older white. So my maximum stock of
"White Wines to Drink" might be 1 per week $\times$ 13 weeks
= 13 bottles of early-drinking whites.

Red Wines. Use the rule for "Red Wines to Drink" for whites,
unless your personal taste differs. I drink very little in this
category, so to continue the example, we'll use one bottle
per week for a three-month period, or thirteen bottles.

Short-Term Wines (One to Three Years):

White wines. This category will compose the larger part
of your white wine stock, usually at the rate of a bottle
per week; 1 bottle per week = 52 bottles per year $\times$ 2
years = 104 bottles, or 9 cases.

Red wines. The same formula: 104 bottles.

85

Medium-Term Wines (Three to Seven Years):

White wines. This is an awkward category for whites. Let's say 1 bottle per month = 12 bottles per year × 5 years = 60 bottles, or 5 cases.

Red wines. This category will probably make up the most important part of your stock, as it covers most red wine styles. Count on 1 bottle a week × 52 weeks = 52 per year × 5 years = 260 bottles, or 22 cases.

Long-Term Wines (Seven to Ten Years and More):

White wines. Let's assume that you drink one bottle a month of a Grand Cru Burgundy or a sweet white. You'll arrive at 12 bottles per year × 10 years = 120 bottles, or 10 cases.

Red wines. Your red wine consumption in this category would ideally be the greatest, but realistically, these more-expensive wines are opened at an average of two per month. Thus 2 bottles per month × 12 months = 24 bottles per year × 10 years = 240 bottles, or 20 cases.

> Total bottles of white: 297
> Total bottles of red: 617
> TOTAL: 958 bottles

Note: This is only a sample. It is imperative that you reconstruct this exercise using your own proportions.

Formula #2

This is called the "party" method of calculation, since Formula #1 assumes that you are sitting home drinking alone, except for an occasional guest! Try to figure out how many dinner parties you give with eight guests (let's say 12 parties $\times$ 8 = 96); how many dinners with four guests (let's say 36 dinners $\times$ 4 = 144); and how many romantic tête-à-têtes (let's say 60 $\times$ 2 = 120) you have in a year. If you assume that each person drinks a half a bottle, and you have people traipsing through your home at the above rates, then using this formula, 360 guests per year $\times$ $^{1}/_{2}$ bottle = 180 bottles.[6]

Formula #3

This formula gives you a simpler way to plan your long-term wine purchases. Assume that you want to be able to drink three top red wines per month ten years from now. You should thus buy 36 bottles every year, so that in ten years you will have 360 bottles of these wines (minus those you opened for testing). The same principle holds true for medium-term wines. If you wish to have a decent stock on hand of a wine that needs five years to mature, buy 36 bottles per year for five years to reach a total of 180 bottles.

87

HOW MUCH IS THIS GOING TO COST?

"Wine and wenches empty men's purses."
—English proverb

Obviously, it is difficult to put an exact price on any given wine, because its value will change each year with the success or distress of the harvest; too, a particular

6. Jacqueline Gardan. *Livre de Cave: Collection Le Bec et La Plume* (Paris: Porphyre Editeur, 1996): 7–8.

bottle's price increases or decreases each year according to supply and demand. Still, there are guidelines. You know that wines intended for immediate or early consumption are less expensive than wines made for more serious cellaring, and you should choose the proportions of wines that you buy according to your budget. It is a safer bet to compose the larger part of your cellar around medium-price, medium-term wines.

Let's take Formula #1 as an example, and use average price estimates. These can obviously be only very rough estimates, because wine market prices fluctuate from source to source, month to month, and country to country. Don't forget that this cellar is bought over time according to a schedule you decide. And don't forget that the total sum here includes enough wines for ten years or more of drinking. With that perspective, the following is a reasonable investment.

88

13 bottles of early-drinking whites × $4 per bottle = $52

13 bottles of early-drinking reds × $5 per bottle = $65

104 bottles of short-term whites × $8 per bottle = $832

104 bottles of short-term reds × $10 per bottle = $1,040

60 bottles of medium-term whites × $18 per bottle = $1,080

260 bottles of medium-term reds × $20 per bottle = $5,200

120 bottles of long-term whites × $35 per bottle = $4,200

240 bottles of long-term reds × $40 per bottle = $9,600

TOTAL: $22,069

It is only the bottles from the early-drinking and short-term categories that are going to require an immediate cash output. The categories of later-aging wines are bought a case at a time, gradually, thus lessening your

immediate expenses. The $22,069 figure is the hypo-
thetical cost of a staggered-maturation-date collection
containing roughly a thousand bottles, bought over a
period of time. You may only drink two hundred bottles in
a year, so you have, theoretically, four or five years to purchase the other eight hundred bottles (which are not of
the original thousand).

A "READY-TO-DRINK" SAMPLE CELLAR

Here is an exercise that might help you build your own
cellar. Below is a cellar put together by a top London wine
merchant. I have included the vintage years so that you
may more easily calculate your own purchases. Let's
assume that we are basing our "staggering" cellar on the
year 1997. I'm going to go through and break down each
category. All you'll have to do then is replace each of the
listed wines below with a case of the wine of your choice
from the appropriate category; drink-now, short-, medium-,
and long-term wines. (Assume all quantities are one twelve-
bottle case.)

RED BORDEAUX
1988 Château Calon-Ségur, St-Estèphe
1988 Château Gruaud-Larose, St-Julien
1988 Château Pichon-Longueville, Comtesse de Lalande,
    Pauillac
1989 Château Léoville-Poyferré, St-Julien
1989 Château Montrose, St-Estèphe
    (Replace with nine-year-old, long-term Bordeaux or equiv-
    alent to drink now or for another three to ten years or
    more, depending.)
1990 Château Haut-Bages Monpelou, Pauillac
1990 Château Fombrauge, St-Emilion

1990 Château Batailley, Pauillac

1990 Château Palmer, Margaux

1990 Château La Mission-Haut-Brion, Pessac-Léognan
(Replace with seven-year-old, long-term Bordeaux or equivalent to drink in three to five years.)

1993 Château Clinet, Pomerol

1993 Cos d'Estournel, St-Estèphe

1993 Château Haut-Brion, Pessac-Léognan

1994 Château Haut-Bailly, Pessac-Léognan

1994 Château Léoville-Barton, St-Julien

1994 Château l'Angélus, Pomerol
(Replace with recent vintages of long-term Bordeaux or equivalent to drink in ten years.)

WHITE BORDEAUX (SWEET)

1991 Château Doisy-Védrines, Barsac
(Replace with a five-year-old, long-term sweet white to drink now and later.)

RED BURGUNDY

1993 Côte de Nuits-Villages, Domaine Ambroise

1993 Gevrey-Chambertin, Domaine Mortet

1993 Pommard, Grand Clos des Epenots, Domaine de Courcel

1993 Beaune Clos des Mouches, Maison Joseph Drouhin
(Replace with four-year-old, medium- and long-term red Burgundies or equivalent to drink in three years and in eight years, respectively—the Pommard and Gevrey being in the long-term category.)

WHITE BURGUNDY

1993 Meursault, Grands Charrons, Domaine Bouzereau

1993 Puligny-Montrachet, Louis Carillon & Fils
(Replace with four-year-old, long-term white Burgundy to drink in three years and later.)

RED RHÔNE
1991 St-Joseph, Clos de Cuminaille, P. Gaillard
1991 Hermitage, M. Chapoutier
>   (Replace with six-year-old, medium-term red Rhône or
>   equivalent for immediate and short-term consumption.)

SPAIN
1991 Pesquera, Reserva, Bodegas Alejandro Fernandez
>   (Replace with a six-year-old, long-term Spanish reserve or
>   equivalent for immediate consumption and short-term cel-
>   laring.)

UNITED STATES
1991 Qupé Syrah, Bien Nacido Vineyard
1991 Hedges Red Mountain Reserve, Cabernet/Merlot
>   (Replace with six-year-old, medium-term reds for immedi-
>   ate consumption.)

AUSTRALIA
1992 Penfold's Bin 707 Cabernet Sauvignon
1992 Yarra Yering Dry Red No. 1
>   (Replace with five-year-old, medium-term reds for imme-
>   diate consumption.)

VINTAGE PORT
1977 Gould Campbell
1980 Dow's Port, Silva & Cosens Ltd.
>   (Replace with older-vintage, long-term ports for immedi-
>   ate and continual consumption!)

This cellar gives you thirty-two cases, or 384 bottles, of which
seven cases are for immediate consumption, twelve are for
medium-term consumption, and eleven are for long-term cellaring—just about the right proportions.

Where to Start

Most of us cannot just walk into a wine merchant, plot a cellar, and walk out with a complete collection. If you can't invest a lot of money up front, and you're still in the experimental stage of learning your likes and dislikes, start by buying one case of a recent-vintage, long-term wine, such as a California Reserve Cabernet Sauvignon, or a top-growth Bordeaux. If you can manage to buy a case of long-term wine every two to three months, and you don't touch it (!), you'll be well on your way to stocking your cellar.

Then try to buy one case, also every two months, of a recent-vintage, medium-range wine, perhaps a California Merlot or a Reserve Chianti, which can be drunk both shortly after purchase and through the next seven years; this adds a lot of flexibility to your collection. For your daily drinking, buy a case each of an inexpensive, light red and white every month—or, better yet, keep a few of those box wines in your refrigerator. They have come a long way since the 1970s!

Getting started does not have to be a major investment of time and money. And until you are sure of your tastes, buying wines a case or two at a time will lower your risk of expensive mistakes. Take advantage of any local wine tastings offered by supermarkets or wine merchants before buying. Also, ask your local wine merchant to mix cases for you. For example, you might buy a case of twelve different Cabernet Sauvignons (from different estates of the same region, or even from different countries!) of the same vintage and price range, and conduct tastings at home with friends.

A STARTER CELLAR

This is a cellar that can be put together very easily and inexpensively; it puts an emphasis on domestic wines. The better California wines seem to be hard to get a hold of, and are sometimes more expensive than imported French wines of the same quality—so start with the well-known wines that are more easily available. In the United States, much as in France and other countries, the best producers are the smallest—the ones who don't produce enough cases to cover a national, much less an international, distribution. Only by driving through the back country, tasting and talking to people on site, will you get a real taste of what the region has to offer. As far as imports are concerned, try to stay away from the large importing companies and brands; they provide consistent value, but not always great distinction, and their wines don't always hold up to serious cellaring, because they've been prepared for mass distribution (by refining, filtering, stabilizing, and so on). There's very little substance left to them. Instead, try to buy as many château-style wines as possible for your cellar—they will be a better investment. I hope that the suggested prices below come close to the retail prices you would find locally. They are based on recent vintages, yet will vary 10 to 25 percent—up or down—by vintage, availability, and the source or purchase, depending on where you live and where you buy them.

93

LONG-TERM REDS (CHOOSE ONE CASE)
Quilceda Creek, Cabernet Sauvignon, Washington ($28)
Caymus Cabernet Sauvignon, Napa ($20)

Luciano Sandrone Barolo Cannubi Boschis, Italy ($46)

Flora Springs Cabernet Sauvignon Stags' Leap District, Napa
($17)

E. et M. Guigal Hermitage, Rhône Valley ($35)

Clos du Val, Cabernet Sauvignon Reserve, Napa ($30)

LONG-TERM WHITES (CHOOSE ONE CASE)

Verget Puligny-Montrachet Sous le Puits, Burgundy ($38)

Domaines Schlumberger Gewurztraminer Grand Cru Kessler,
Alsace ($25)

Château Suduiraut, Sauternes ($60)

Kistler Chardonnay, Sonoma Valley ($38)

MEDIUM-TERM REDS (CHOOSE TWO CASES)

Leonetti Cabernet Sauvignon, Washington ($29)

Hess Collection Cabernet Sauvignon, Napa ($18)

Au Bon Climat Pinot Noir Santa Barbara County Bien Nacido
Vineyard ($25)

Caves Alianca, Douro Foral Garrafeira, Portugal ($16)

Bodegas Ismael Arroyo Ribera del Duero Mesoneros de
Castilla Crianza, Spain ($14)

Domaine G. Roumier Bonnes Mares, Burgundy ($45)

Groth Cabernet Sauvignon, Napa ($20)

Domaine Michel Lafarge Volnay, Clos des Chenes, Burgundy
($60)

Ridge Zinfandel, Sonoma Valley, Pagani Ranch ($20)

MEDIUM-TERM WHITES (CHOOSE TWO CASES)

Ferrari-Carano Chardonnay, Alexander Valley ($20)

Château Ste. Michelle Chardonnay Columbia Valley Château
Reserve ($22)

Wynns Chardonnay Coonawarra, Australia ($12)

Domaine Denis Gaudry Pouilly-Fumé Coteaux du Petit
Boisgibault, Loire ($16)

SHORT-TERM REDS (CHOOSE ONE CASE)
Château Bonnet, Bordeaux Vieilli en Futs de Chene ($8)
Château Brown Lamartine, Bordeaux Supérieur ($12)
Nozzole Chianti Classico Riserva, Italy ($12)
Château Dalina Merlot Russe, Bulgaria ($4)
Clos du Bois Merlot, Sonoma ($10)
Casa Lapostolle, Cabernet Sauvignon, Colchagua, Chile ($9)
Domaine de la Coste, Coteaux du Languedoc ($8)
Château de Gourgazaud, Minervois ($8)
Montes Cabernet Sauvignon, Curico, Chile ($8)
Beringer Zinfandel, Napa ($9)

SHORT-TERM WHITES (CHOOSE ONE CASE)
Drayton's Chardonnay Hunter Valley, Australia ($8)
Robert Mondavi Chardonnay, Central Coast ($11)
Camelot Chardonnay, Santa Barbara County ($12)
Snoqualmie Johannisberg Riesling, Columbia Valley,
    Washington ($6)
Van Duzer Riesling Dry Oregon Reserve ($8)
Plus . . . one case of a vintage Champagne or sparkling wine.

95

THE FRENCH CELLAR

60 Bottles for $600.00
With a little hunting through your local discount wine stores, supermarkets, and catalogs, you should be able to find quite a few beauties for everyday drinking. The following is a simple cellar formula that can be acquired rather quickly and affordably, and which is meant for immediate or short-term consumption.

Bordeaux—20 bottles
• A few *cru classés* in Saint-Julien or Saint-Estèphe
• Several Saint-Emilion or Pomerol (for their Merlot)
• Some Graves

Burgundy—10 bottles
- Five bottles of white, such as Chablis, Chassagne-Montrachet, or the lesser known Ladoix, Saint-Romain, Maconnais
- Five bottles of red from regional appellations such as Rully, Mercurey, Côtes de Nuits, and Côtes de Beaume

Alsace—6 bottles
- Two Riesling
- Two Pinot Gris
- Two Gewurztraminer

Loire Valley—6 bottles
- Reds—Chinon or Saumur
- Whites—Muscadet or Sancerre

Côte du Rhône—6 bottles
- Two Côte-Rotie
- Two Gigondas
- Two Châteauneuf-du-Pape

Southwest and Languedoc-Roussillon—6 bottles
- One of two liquoreux (sweet wines)
- Several solid reds from Cahors, Bergerace, Buzet, or Madiran
- Several vins de pays from Languedoc-Roussillon

Provence—4 bottles
- Two Bandol
- Two red Côtes de Provence

Sparkling—2 bottles
- A cheap champagne (but, ugh, you run a risk here!), or,
- One Crémant de Bourgogne
- One Crémant de Limoux

CHAPTER 4

FINDING AND BUYING WINE

"Wine drinkers never make artists."

—Gratinos, 5 B.C.

*T*racking down a wine once you've decided you want to try it or buy it is often the most difficult part of building your collection. Supermarkets, chain wine shops, and independent wine specialty shops are the easiest places to make a start. But with the confusing distribution laws in the United States, a wine distributed in another region may not be available in yours. Also, if you take a look at a *Beverage Media* (the bible of U.S. distributors, listing by region all distributors and their brands), you'll notice that pretty much all of the large national distributors and importers bring in the same wines. This is obviously due to volume sales, and means that it is not profitable for smaller foreign estates to export their wine. For domestic wine availability, get a copy of *Wines and Vines Buyer's Guide*, which has a complete listing of all U.S. wineries, brands, trade associations, and distributors.

The result is that almost every wine collector in America buys the same top-end Bordeaux and ends up with the same cellar! So where do you go for a little variety, and what are your other options?

THE WINE MERCHANT OR SPECIALTY STORE

If you can find a reliable wine shop close to your home, you could be in an ideal situation. Establish a rapport with a merchant you trust, who knows your tastes and your budget, and you're on your way. A good merchant will not only guide you but also help you find the wines you are looking for and, eventually, store them for a charge. A merchant is also likely to have a number of wines in the midprice range as well as access to older vintages. Specialty shops also do a lot of the work for you; most have a bin of some "Best Buys," wines that they've found to have a good price:quality ratio. Such shops will also be there for you after the sale of a wine. If you have a problem with a particular case or bottle, a good merchant will take care of it for you, either by replacing the wine or giving you a credit.

The only negative of a specialty store is the possibility of higher prices—you'll have to pay for all of that special attention and service! Also, since such shops usually have a single owner, you risk having your choices influenced or limited by the owner's personal taste and professional knowledge. If the owner happens to dislike German wines and have a penchant for the Rhône Valley, the advice you receive may not be wholly objective.

THE CHAIN WINE STORES

Here, the problem may be the inverse! You will find practically the same selection of wine in all of a chain's branches, and a less original selection of wines, as the

98

goal is to please a larger group of tastes. Also, a chain's more generic wines may be less expensive, but it makes up for this by marking up considerably its profit margins on luxury, or finer, wines.

The advantage of a chain store—which is halfway between an independent shop and a supermarket—is that you can have the intimacy of individual attention and advice from a merchant or cavist, yet also benefit from lower prices: Chains have powerful buying centers and obtain most of their midrange wines in bulk, then pass the savings on to you. For this same reason, you can count on a reliable stock and selection of wine.

THE SUPERMARKET OR HYPERMARKET

The supermarket may very well do for you if you know what you want and what you are doing. You have the advantage of discount prices, a large choice, and a number of inexpensive wines. But pay attention: You don't know how the wine has been treated or stored. I probably would not buy a serious wine from a supermarket, even if the price was irresistible.

99

Other disadvantages are many: There is rarely a wine specialist on hand, the selection leans heavily toward mass-produced wines and négociants, the promotions feature less important vintages more frequently than greater ones, and you will find many inconsistencies among the prices and the availability of wines.

And again, watch carefully for improper storage conditions. Steer far away from bottles that have been standing upright under a lighted display! The store may tell you that its turnover is so high that the bottles don't have time to become damaged—but don't always believe it. The best merchants treat their wines like their own and display even the less expensive wines on their sides, away from heat and light.

WINE CLUBS AND CATALOGUES

Wine clubs, whose members order by mail, usually offer the what amateur special promotions, information about each wine and its producer in a newsletter, and the opportunity to participate in local group wine tastings and meetings. You have the convenience of having the wine delivered directly to your home, instructive catalogues, clear and competitive tariffs, and, often, the chance to buy *en primeur* (before the wine is bottled). Clubs also encourage you to purchase mixed cases—each case holds several different wines. This allows you to taste a selection of different wines without having to commit to buying each in bulk yet still benefit from a volume discount. Most merchants allow this practice as well, but the advantage of a wine club is that it places more emphasis on it. Clubs are concerned with helping members learn about wines, which encourages repeat business.

The disadvantages include the lack of an original selection. Clubs usually offer only the best-known wines, because these are the easiest and surest to sell! Also, because club offers are so interesting that they are often sold out by the time you make your order. You can find local wine clubs in your newspaper, in the classified sections of wine magazines, and through wine stores and merchants.

THE AUCTION HOUSE—GOING ... GOING ... GONE!

Does the idea of sitting in on a commercial wine auction at Sotheby's or Sherry-Lehmann's intimidate you? Do you wonder if a private collector can survive the hustle and bustle and come away with a good buy? The answer is yes—if you do your homework first. The mistake that most auctiongoers make is not studying the auction catalog beforehand. You must know what you want and how much you are willing to spend on it before it comes on the stand, or under the hammer. Otherwise, you might be overwhelmed by the rapid-fire bidding.

In American auctions, the rarest luxury wines usually go to the retail buyers with the highest bid—often far higher than the prices found in retail stores. So set your sights instead on second- or third-growth Bordeaux or lesser vintages. Also, because of the relative international indifference to American wines, auctions can be good places to pick up some domestic bargains.

If you have the money, the auction house is the best place for finding rare bottles and rare vintages. If what is up for offer can be found in normal commerce, however, the auction house might prove more costly than profitable. Remember, if you are a high roller and things get out of hand, as sometimes they do when you find yourself caught up in the excitement, you can always choose to bid by telephone or fax to protect yourself from impulsive paddle waving—which could cost you your house.

The most important advantage of buying at an auction is the guarantee of quality. Auctions master are usually wine experts, and quite expert at that. Not only are they versed in the art of winemaking and tasting, but they could be considered historians as well. They are backed by an entire team of professionals, who inspect the wines, taste them, and determine their value and opening bid.

Selling Your Wine at Auction

The guarantee of quality that buying from an auction

house gives you is directly related to the care taken when such houses buy the wines or collections that they are going to auction off. Before buying from a private collector, they want to know how long the wine has been held, from where it was obtained, and so on.

For example, the climate that the collector lives in can affect the wine's valuation: Some regions are more humid or dry than others, and therefore their cellaring conditions are deemed more stable or unstable. Auction houses look for the telltale signs of a wine's condition. A wine bottle with a damaged label is harder to sell, especially if it's faded, which might mean that the wine was stored in too much light. The level of wine in the bottle is also a clue to its condition or quality: Too little indicates excessive evaporation or a leaky cork.

If you are thinking about selling off some of your collection, forget all simple table wines, off vintages, and bottles in poor condition, despite their content. A good way to try to estimate the value of what you have is to call, ask for an auction catalogue, and compare. When you approach an auction house for an estimate, or request of sale, give it as much information about your wines as you can: vintages, condition, where, how, and when you obtained them, how they were stored (in bins or in original wooden cases?), and the number of bottles you have (partial lot or full lot?). You might even send a few photos of your cellar; this could pique the house's interest enough for it to send its inspectors.

Storage conditions are the top priority. Most auction houses will automatically reject wines that have been stored in aboveground cellars that are not temperature and humidity controlled. And forget anything that was stored at room temperature. Those wines kept in cellars south of the Mason Dixon line are subjected to a heightened scrutiny, as this famous line dividing Pennsylvania and Maryland not only divided the free from the slave states during the Civil War, but also marks an important climatic difference between North and South. Any wines stored south of this line may have been exposed to excessive humidity and higher temperatures.

HOW TO KNOW WHAT'S AVAILABLE ON THE MARKET

If you have a particular wine in mind, you can ask your local merchant. He or she will consult a book called the *Beverage Media* or *Beverage Buyer*. These are guides that list all of the nation's distributors and the wines that they import; each region of the United States has its own edition. Some distributors are independent and so have unique selections of wines. Others are national and have outlets in all major cities, which generally carry the same wines, although some outlets may adapt their selections to regional preferences.

Beverage Media and *Beverage Buyer* are quarterly guidebooks available only to professionals, because they usually list wholesale or bulk prices. If you want a look at one yourself, though, ask your merchant if you might look at an old copy from the previous quarter (keep in mind that the wines available might already have changed in that period). If you do not have a liquor license, your merchant may deny your request, but persist and explain that you are only curious and researching future purchases.

You can also contact the source from which you learned about the wine, by calling a wine magazine or newspaper, for example. You may be put in touch with the journalist who wrote the piece and/or the wine pro-

103

ducer directly. Restaurants may also help you purchase wines you discovered from their wine lists.

Wines Unavailable in the United States

If the wine you want is not available in the United States, you can contact the producer directly and try to arrange an order through a local distributor, or pay the price of having a shipment made to you. Wine clubs and mail-order companies are other very good options. At the end of this book you will find an appendix list of useful wine agencies, institutes, and governmental organizations that can help you track down a wine. Some of the institutes—Wines from Spain, for instance—can provide you with a list of wines available in the U.S. matched with their corresponding distributors.

Direct Buying

Buying directly from a producer or property is by far the most agreeable way to stock your cellar. Nothing replaces tasting a wine in its own environment, with the winemaker by your side, explaining the long and difficult birth of the prodigy child. It's a touching experience that might even add a little magic to the wine. I can't tell you how many times I've traveled to Italy and either fallen under the spell of a winemaker's smooth Latin charm, or succumbed to heatstroke, then returned home with my wine and opened it before a group of coworkers or friends to whom I had been boasting and raving madly—only to find the actual tasting very anticlimactic, and even to hear someone mutter, "Guess you had to be there, huh?"

The traditions and formalities of buying wine on the property vary according to country and even by region within a country. Take Napa Valley, for example, the Disneyland of wine-producing regions . . . organized tours, gift shops with T-shirts and souvenirs, museums, picnic sites . . . everything needed to greet the curious wine amateur or the more informed collector. Most wineries here don't require an invitation or a reservation, and traveling wine lovers can comfortably taste and experiment at their own rhythm. (Usually two visits in the morning and two visits in the afternoon—spitting required—is a good pace.) If you are a more serious connoisseur planning to buy, you can call or write the owner ahead of time to ask for a private tasting or meeting.

This is not at all the case with most European wine regions, however. If you're in Bordeaux for your summer vacation and happen to drive past Château d'Yquem, don't bother knocking on the door for a visit, even if your intention is to purchase. Most top-classified growths in Bordeaux cannot be sold directly to the public anyway; they must pass through a négociant. In both Burgundy and Bordeaux you will find some châteaux open only by appointment—and the request must be written. Still, regions such as Champagne, the Loire Valley, and Alsace (the latter only recently) are far more open to receiving visitors. These are better places to start your wine-shopping tour of France.

Tasting one-on-one with the owner or winemaker of the château may be interesting, but it is also demanding. You have to know what you are talking about, how to taste, and what questions to ask (climatic conditions of a particular vintage, yields, vinification methods, and so on). But even more important is to not let yourself become influenced by the surroundings or the romantic selling pitch of the vintner. Sometimes the anonymity of a tour group can be helpful: You can from your own impressions and decisions, but have someone nearby to answer any questions.

Also, don't be too intimidated. If you feel that a squat, leathery little man is staring you down as you taste his wines, don't hesitate to take a look at his equipment—his winemaking equipment, that is. The tasting glasses should be clean and clearly wiped, the barrels maintained, and the pressing machine immaculate; the state of a machine of this importance is usually indicative of his overall work habits. Don't be afraid to ask about unfamiliar or bothersome odors. If you like the wines and find the price fair, you would be expected to buy something. On the other hand, if you don't like the wines, or find the price not appropriate to the wines' quality, you are expected to say so. If you wish to really engage the winemaker in an animated conversation and perhaps ingratiate yourself to the point of receiving a sample bottle, ask him why his wine is better than his neighbors', then sit down and get comfortable for what might be a very long discussion.

How to Get It Home

Obviously, if you're touring the American wine regions by car, you can fill up your trunk with bottles and go home. Unfortunately, the same is not true for overseas shopping. Indeed, it's almost more trouble and expense than it's worth to buy wine in quantity and have it shipped home. First of all, most small estates in Europe are not equipped to handle small international orders with all their customs forms and paperwork. The U.S. laws allow one liter of alcoholic beverage to be imported if you are twenty-one years of age or older, if it is for you or for a gift, and if it is not in violation of the laws of your state. Alcoholic beverages are also subject to federal excise taxes, which generally exceed customs duties: The duty rate for alcohol is 30.9 cents per liter of sparkling wine, and from 8.3 to 26.4 cents per liter for still wine.

So how do collectors get their hands on international wines that are unavailable in the United States or their own countries? One option may be to obtain a private liquor license—although this is impractical for all but the most dedicated collector. A more sensible approach when you have a specific wine in mind is to ask the local distributor or wine merchant with whom you do most of your business to order it for you. You will probably still be expected to pay near-retail prices. This is perfectly legal and very common.

WINE FUTURES: BUYING EN PRIMEUR

Unless you've been following a particular wine's performance for years and feel that you know it inside and out, or you're considering an extremely rare growth, buying wine futures, or commitments to purchase wine before it's bottled, is not always a good idea. This system gives a particular wine trade a two-year cash flow while the wine awaits retail release at (in most cases) higher prices. (I say "in most cases" because many things can happen before the wine leaves its barrels and enters its bottle. For example, currency exchange rates can change.)

Châteaux owners in Bordeaux must keep their wine in barrels for two years before bottling it and placing it on the shelves. Obviously, this is an expensive system that weighs very heavily on a château's cash flow, because it is not at all certain that two years after harvest the wine will sell rapidly and at the best price. The *en primeur* system was established between the châteaux owners (the sellers) and the négociants or wine merchants (buyers) to counteract this risk and provide a little insurance for the châteaux, allowing them to continue barrel and bottle aging.

When a château offers its wine *en primeur,* one or several *brokers de place* ("wine brokers") are called upon; their responsibility is to divvy up the wines among the wine merchants with whom the château has chosen to work. It is the broker who negotiates the wine's price with the merchant. In the past, when the system was ruled by the wine merchants, the brokers had an even more important role. Because they were particularly well informed as to the wine's quality and, especially, the owners' financial difficulties, the brokers could allow the wine merchants to buy the best wine, at the best price, at the best moment.

The economic crisis of the 1970s weakened the wine merchants of Bordeaux, and since then it has generally been the owners who have dictated the law. They choose their wine merchants and, most important, the number of cases that will be allocated. It is the owners, too who determine the wine's price.

Is this a subtle form of blackmail between the owners and the wine merchants? The wine merchant does have the choice of saying yes or no to the owner's allocation and price designation. But woe betide he who says no and thus bars himself forever from that owner's list of wine merchants—because no second chance will be given. Very rare indeed are those wine merchants who have the power to refuse the dictates of an owner; even the largest wine merchants often have no choice but to accept the quantity of wine at the price imposed by the owner. It is then up to them to sell the wine, with the widest possible margin that they dare, to make their profits.

This situation is rather perverse, but everyone involved somehow makes do with its advantages and disadvantages. No owner knows where or to whom the wines are finally sold: This is the trump card of the wine merchants, who preciously keep their operations to themselves.

Only the owners decide at what price they will sell their wines. For a measuring stick, they use the price at which the neighbors' crus are sold, along with the capital gains on the market—in other words, the profit margins that wine merchants set aside for themselves, made both on the *primeurs* and on the price trends for previous vintages. The quality of their wine or, more precisely, the idea they have of the future quality of their wine, has no true effect on the price. The reputation of the vintage year, however, is of far more importance. A highly publicized vintage will sell for more than a vintage about which everyone has doubts.

Some crus always sell at higher prices than others; this is simply a question of notoriety. The hierarchy among the crus is very real; it corresponds to the prestige of the bottle label in relation to market demand. If a cru proves to be a little too pretentious, raising the price of the vintage but failing to sell it, it is nearly impossible for it to recover from the damage to its reputation.

To avoid complete and total pricing mayhem, which has been known to damage both owners and wine merchants, a remedy was concocted: divide the *en primeur* "process" into lots, or *tranches*. The price of a cru's first offering is considered the *première tranche*, or price at which the owner agrees to sell the wine, in a limited quantity, to test the water. The quantity of the *tranche* depends upon both the reputation of the cru and the strategy of the particular owner. The owner of a cru that is in a strong position, such as a premier cru classé, knows that the label his bottle is wearing will create such a demand that the second lot of bottles can be sold at an even higher price. This second lot is usually offered a month after the first, and usually exceeds the first's prices by 20 or 30 percent. If the demand is there, the wine will sell.

HOW TO READ A WINE LABEL

Reading a wine label, as well as the harvest report, will give you important background information. The glossary at the end of the book provides explanation of other languages that may appear on a label. Here are two examples of a Portuguese white and a German white:

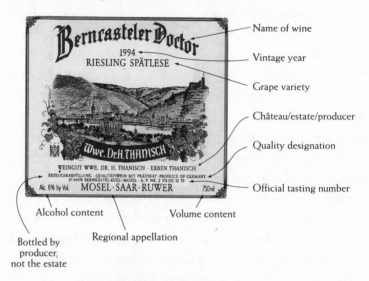

Name of wine

Vintage year

Grape variety

Château/estate/producer

Quality designation

Official tasting number

Volume content

Alcohol content

Regional appellation

Bottled by producer, not the estate

110

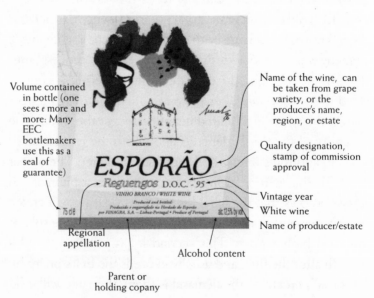

Volume contained in bottle (one sees *e* more and more: Many EEC bottlemakers use this as a seal of guarantee)

Name of the wine, can be taken from grape variety, or the producer's name, region, or estate

Quality designation, stamp of commission approval

Vintage year

White wine

Name of producer/estate

Regional appellation

Alcohol content

Parent or holding copany

On the other hand, the owner of a lesser-known or less reputable cru could very well have problems selling its *première tranche* and will be only too happy to get the same sale conditions for the remaining lots. Added to this spiral of price game is the arbitrary judgments of certain wine critics. It only takes a wine writer to praise a particular wine and its demand curve, as well as its price curve, can take a dramatic upswing.

When you buy the grands crus *en primeur,* you know that they will be delivered only eighteen months later. But you are not buying directly from the châteaux, because the majority sell their production only through wine distributors. It is therefore the wine distributor who actually proposes *en primeur* wine sales, after adding a margin to their acquisition price (see the following chart, which lists the purchase and resale prices obtained by one wine merchant in Bordeaux for his 1995 *primeurs*). You buy from a wine merchant, who originally bought from a distributor, who bought from a château. But the merchant may not be able to guarantee that in eighteen months' time, he will be able to come up with the goods. Should he fail to pay the château for its wine, the château will not deliver. This unfortunate scenario has happened, and will happen again, despite the fact that most merchants and distributors are respectable traders.

Often a wine that has been offered *en primeur* has not even been tasted by the wine merchant. Not even the largest companies conduct formal presale tastings, because they are counting on the bottle label to sell the wine. The distributors have a pretty good idea of the relative quality between each cru, but it is often in their best interests to keep mum and not share their opinion with the owner or the wine merchant; indeed, the most important quality of a good distributor (acting as a broker) is knowing how to keep quiet. When *en primeur* tastings do take place, always toward the end of March, they are criticized by the owners, who claim that their wines will not do well at this early stage; wine merchants and journalists likewise wonder if the proposed samples are accurate representations of the future blends. And don't forget that the tasting conditions under which these sessions are conducted are always precarious.

The risks concerning the quality of a wine sold *en primeur* are numerous and all too real. So given all my advice and forewarning, should you buy *en primeur?* The answer, for the experienced collector, is more yes than no. Buying *en primeur* allows you to purchase the best-known crus at the most reasonable prices. Buying *en primeur* is often the only way to procure a cru for your cellar, because these wines are often unavailable through normal distribution channels.

Good deals, then, are within your reach. All you need to do is to follow attentively the harvest reports and analyses of the appellations that interest you. Then choose a strategy: You can either go for the well-known, sure values (the most famous grands crus) or bet on some long shots that, if well calculated, will bring you a better price:quality ratio.[7]

THE COST OF WINE

Before investing your hard-earned money into a wine for your collection, examine the question of how much it costs. I've already discussed great wines, and the fact that better wines require care that is more expensive. But what

7. Jacques Sallé. "Should We Buy 1995 Bordeaux en Primeur?" *Vintage* 7 (Autumn 1996): 14–16.

WINES TO BUY *EN PRIMEUR**

Classed Growth and good bourgeois red Bordeaux
Classed Growth Sautnernes
Northern Rhône reds and whites
Red and white Burgundy from a reliable producer
Vintage Ports
Vintage Champagne
New-style Cabernet Sauvignons and Vini da Tavola from
   Tuscany

*Source: Oz Clarke, *The Essential Wine Book,* Simon & Schuster, 1988, p. 17.

does it really cost? Wine is the focus of a unique trade. The markets for great wines, good wines, and simple wines each has its own law of exchange.

A great wine with an international reputation will be the object of strong demand; it will become progressively rarer and more expensive. Take the case of Château Haut-Brion—one of the first great wines to be exported. Its reputation is secure, it was classified as a premier grand cru in 1855, and it has managed to sustain such a high level of quality and prestige that it heads the list of desirable purchases. It has become very expensive and rare.

What are the chances for wines that have no great fame, for which demand is low? Logic states that their prices must be attractive if they are to tempt the customer in search of discoveries.

So how much does a bottle of wine cost? Let's begin with everything except the wine: The empty bottle, cork, label, and seal, together with the packing case and labor cost, add up to more than 75 cents per bottle. Again, the model used is a French one. These prices will vary and should only be considered a general guideline.

113

Along with this, the total cost of growing, winemaking, and depreciation per hectare of vines is rarely less than $7,500 per year. If yields are normal (around fifty hectoliters of wine per hectare), the unit cost of the wine is $1.15 per 75cl bottle. If yields are very low—from old vines, for example—the quantity is halved and the cost of the bottle's contents approximately doubled, to $2.25. Conversely, that cost is reduced by half if the vines produce twice as much wine. The total cost per bottle can thus vary between $1.32 and $3.00, depending on yields; that is the heart of the matter. And if we add the cost of maturing in new barrels (each barrel costs $560 and holds 225 liters), replaced every three years, we must add 63 cents per bottle—plus additional labor costs. The price per bottle thus rises to more than $3.75, even without marketing costs. Wines from a single *terroir* can therefore cost between $1.32 and $5.62!

But they will not be the same wines. The former will be modest, light, probably diluted. The lack of natural sugar will be made up for by the addition of beet sugar (this is known as chaptalization); to give the excessive yield a little more dressing up, the fermentation will be operated with the aid of aromatic yeasts in temperature-controlled stainless-steel vats. This kind of wine can be made more or less anywhere in the world, and certain vineyards achieve production costs so low that they can sell a reasonable wine (not good, but not bad) at prices that defy all competition.

But establishments that are not famous, and cannot sell their production at a sufficiently high price, have no choice but to employ winemaking methods that increase yield and decrease quality. The winemaker has to produce a little more wine, at a slightly lower price, to meet commitments.

Faced with this price-versus-quality dilemma (where the price determines the quality), there is little room for the authentic craftsman-winemaker who respects the vines and has a fierce determination to let the soil express itself through modest yields. By failing to adapt to the market, the full diversity of traditional, natural wines is doomed; and the craftsman will be seen as an adventurer, on the margins of our cash-worshipping world.[8]

THE WORLD'S MOST EXPENSIVE WINES

Here, for your curiosity, are some of the world's most expensive wines (from Michel Dovaz's *Livre d'Or*). They all have a retail value exceeding $500 per bottle. These wines are out of time, out of the market. It is no accident that year after year, decade after decade, these same wines make this list. You can assume this is because people believe that they are worth their prices; that they have stood the test of time. These truly great wines have attained universal recognition, by all palates and appreciations. They would win a place of honor in any cellar—but very rarely come onto the market; your best bet is auctions. Keep your eyes peeled for these.

Scharzhofberg TBA
Weingut Egon Müller
Ruwer, Germany
Yearly production: 200–300 bottles per year in years
      produced: 1959, 1971, 1975, 1976, 1989, 1990,
      and 1994

La Romanée-Conti
Domaine de La Romanée-Conti
La romanée-conti Grand Cru (Burgundy), France
Yearly production: 6,000 bottles

Eiswein Bernkasteler Doktor TBA
Weingut Witwe Dr. H. Thanisch
Mosel-Saar-Ruwer, Germany
Yearly production: 50,000 bottles

8. Jacques Sallé. "The Costs of Wine: Economic Logic." *Vintage* 7 (Autumn 1996): 51–53.

Wehlener Sonnenuhr TBA
Weingut J. J. Prüm
Mosel-Saar-Ruwer, Germany
Yearly production: 500 bottles

Pétrus
Château Pétrus
Pomerol (Bordeaux), France
Yearly production: 42,000 bottles

Schloss Johannisberg Eiswein
Weingut Schloss Johannisberg
Eiswein, Germany
Yearly production: 200–400 bottles

Hattenheimer Pfaffenberg TBA
Domänenweingut Schloss Schönborn
Rheingau, Germany
Yearly production: 300 bottles

Château d'Yquem
Sauternes Premier Cru Supérieur, France
Yearly production: 60,000 bottles

Maximin Grünhauser Abtsberg TBA
Gutsverwaltung Andreas and Carl von Schubert
Mosel, Germany

Montrachet
Domaine Marquis de Laguiche/Maison Joseph Drouhin
Montrachet Grand Cru (Burgundy), France
Yearly production: 9,000 bottles

La Tâche
Domaine de La Romanée-Conti
La Tâche Grand Cru (Burgundy), France
Yearly production: 20,000 bottles

Erbacher Marcobrunn TBA
Freiherrlich Langwerth von Simmern'sches Rentamt
Rheingau, Germany
Yearly production: 200 bottles

La Turque
E. et M. Guigal
Côte Rôtie (Rhône), France
Yearly production: 8,000 bottles

Clos de Mesnil
Champagne Krug
Champagne, France
Yearly production: 15,000 bottles

Richebourg
Domaine Méo-Camuzet
Richebourg Grand Cru (Burgundy), France
Yearly production: 1,200 bottles

Bollinger Vieilles Vignes Françaises
Champagne Bollinger
Champagne, France
Yearly production: 14,000 bottles

Niederhausen-Schlossböckelheim Schlossböckelheimer
     Kupfergrube TBA
Staatlichen Weinbaudomänen
Nahe, Germany
Yearly production: 250 bottles

Wachenheimer Luginsland TBA
Weingut Dr. Bürklin-Wolf
Rheinpfalz-Palatinat, Germany

La Romanée
Domaine du Château de Vosne-Romanée

> La Romanée Grand Cru (Burgundy), France
> Yearly production: 4,000 bottles
>
> Aszú Essencia
> Tokaji, Hungary

GETTING THE MOST OUT OF YOUR WINE-COLLECTING DOLLARS

To sum up how to best make your wine-collecting dollars stretch:

- Avoid expensive mistakes: Understand what wine is and which are worth cellaring. Don't wait too long to drink young wines and don't drink old ones too early.
- Buy wines you know and have tasted.
- Buy wines that have a track record. If you want a wine for twenty years down the line, buy one that you have tasted when twenty years old.
- For medium-range cellaring, buy smaller, lesser-known foreign and domestic estates.
- Invest in a proper storage area.
- Find a reliable merchant.
- Buy for drinking, not investing.
- Dabble with *en primeur* purchases only if you already have a good idea of a particular château's past price record.
- At auctions, set spending limits, study the catalog before the sale, and attend presale tastings along with as many sales as possible to understand the market.

CHAPTER 5

STORING WINE

"Your stomach is your wine cellar; keep the stock small and cool."

—Charles Tovey

Y ou've decided which wines you want. You've found them and bought them. Now where do you put them? We don't all have the luck of owning an eighteenth-century château with a vaulted cellar. Any wine that is going to be kept for even a few weeks needs to be stored in the correct conditions, and most homes today don't make this easy. So even devoted wine lovers are forced to do without the better growths unless they have access to a cellar and enough space. Which is a great pity—because very little is involved in setting up a cozy little nest for your better bottles. All you need is a few square feet and a bit of imagination.

Basements have been converted into garages, boiler rooms, workshops, and laundries these days, but in the process that essential item, the decent wine cellar, has been overlooked. And real-estate developers have done nothing to remedy the situation, building houses as cheaply as possible, with an underfloor space rather than a cellar.

Though environment is very important for aging wines, most crucial is avoiding light, temperature changes, and vibration. Wines need to be protected from strain. They are generally acknowledged to suffer when in transport, when subject to frequent temperature changes, and when exposed to light; such strains are likely to age them prematurely. Sudden shifts in temperature are also very bad for wine. This is why a refrigerator is wine's worst enemy. To a lesser extent, daily temperature changes also place strain on wine. This does not mean that leaving a wooden box of wine in the corner of the garage will completely ruin it; you will run the risk of accelerating its aging process, however. (Of course there is generally a certain amount of thermal inertia within a box or stack of boxes, but this is not always adequate for wines.)

120

Your main risk is dilation, which may lead to the cork being expelled. If wine is exposed to extreme cold (less than 14 degrees F) for several months, its development may be blocked so that it never opens up properly. Excessive heat also causes irreparable damage to wines: Those shipped in containers through the Tropics, or merely left in the sun of a port warehouse, can be subjected to temperatures of over 122 degrees F. The bottles "weep"—wine seeps out through the cork—and the worst of it is that the wine is permanently damaged by this. Ideally, of course, air-conditioned containers should be used . . . but this shoots up transport costs.

Although the way wine develops in a bottle remains a somewhat mysterious process, it has been proved that temperatures below 41 degrees F and higher than 68 degrees F are a threat to its development. This range leaves lovers of fine wines with a certain latitude, however. Given that the biochemical development of a wine depends equally on the nature of the wine, the passage of time, and, especially, the surrounding temperature, the wine will age more slowly in a 50-degree F environment than in a 68-degree one. The cooler temperatures slow metabolic processes in much the same way a refrigerator keeps food from spoiling as quickly. And, like humans, wine ages best in peace and quiet, with no stress or strain and less likelihood of wrinkles!

A good cellar is still the best way to store and age wine. It provides a very well-insulated setting in terms of temperature, and is dark and damp. The ideal temperature for wine is between 50 and 55 degrees F—relatively low for most cellars. Seasonal variations in temperature also have to be taken into consideration, for while a cellar may reach 59 degrees F in the summer, it may well drop to 50 degrees F in the winter. Still, such differences do not tire a wine too much. Daily temperature swings seem to have a larger, long-term effect on its development. Thus it is a good idea to have a maximum/minimum thermometer on hand to record such shifts, and to try to prevent them by blocking air vents where necessary.

121

The natural humidity of a cellar is also beneficial— not to the wines, but to the corks! Laying bottles on their sides places the wine in contact with the cork and prevents shrinkage at the top. But if there is insufficient outside humidity, the cork may well dehydrate at the top, even if it is protected by a metallic cap. So the more humid the cellar, the better. The disadvantage is that labels tend to go moldy and peel off. To keep them in good condition, coat them with a silicon-based product, such as an aerosol shoe cleaner, or apply a layer of varnish. While humidity does entail mold, especially when air circulation is poor, remember that mold has never adversely affected wine stored in glass bottles properly sealed with corks.

In short, the conditions required for a cellar to be good for wine are not particularly stringent, especially since a large number of them can be modified. Temperature can be controlled with an air-conditioner, and remarkable progress has been made recently in equipment: Hygrometry can be corrected with sand trays full of water, for instance. It is also possible to use just part of an existing cellar by insulating only a few square feet of space. Even if you don't have a cellar, you have several other options; see "Alternatives to Cellars" below.

WHAT ARE IDEAL STORAGE CONDITIONS?

Temperature

Temperature directly affects the evolution of a wine. The warmer the cellar, the faster the wine there is going to evolve. Wines that are stored at high temperatures age rapidly, become tired, and mature poorly. Wines stored at continually fluctuating temperatures become "exhausted" and "overworked" from the repeated adjustments. The longer and cooler the cellar is maintained, the more gradual will be the wine's development, allowing it to reach its fullest potential.

Sound familiar? This is the same principle involved in growing grapes.

It is important to know the temperature of your *cave* and its fluctuations. If you have a refrigeration unit, this is easy. If you have a cellar, invest in a minimum/maximum thermometer and measure the temperature in its every corner. You want to detect drafty spots and the hot spots, so that you can stabilize the temperature of the cellar (by insulating doors leading upstairs, for example). If blocking or insulating sources of heat or cold doesn't suffice, your next step is to install a refrigeration or heating unit. This is costly, and the size of your wine collection may or may not justify the expenditure.

Your cellar temperature can range from 41 to 64 degrees F, but your goal should be somewhere in the middle—50 to 55 degrees. It will probably change temperature from winter to summer, and this won't hurt the wine. But what is important, again, is that this change be made gradually and slowly, and not violently or often. If there are too many fluctuations, your wines will continually expand and contract in their bottles, their corks will weaken, and the wines will ultimately leak around the corks, leaving a thick, syrupy residue.

Humidity

The relative humidity desired in a cellar is about 75 percent (and no more than 85 percent). Why? Because you want things humid enough to keep the corks wet, yet not so humid that your wine labels fall apart and your equipment rusts or rots.

I have a French friend whose grandfather had been collecting since 1930, and had bottles that were far older than that. The wines had been carefully placed in the cellar of the family's country house on the northern coast of France. After his grandfather's death, my friend inherited the cellar and went to investigate the condition of the wines. He found wine cartons so humid that they had rotted and fallen apart, spilling their bottles out onto the floor. Among the oldest bottles (which had been set aside in a special corner) the labels were long gone, and he had no idea what was what—a true historical loss. Those bottles that were identifiable, and that we opened, had picked up the rotting odors of the *cave* and were undrinkable. It turned out that the only bottles that had survived in drinkable condition were the fifty or so that had been tucked away and forgotten in an upstairs bedroom closet! There's no point in having a cellar if it's not the right one.

So how do you get rid of humidity? Drying the area artificially will only serve as a short-term solution. Instead, try to find the cause. Usually this is a humid wall or floor, and the solution is easy and inexpensive: Cover walls with resin or liquid rubber, and cement flooring with a layer of polyurethane or dry sand, which absorbs humidity.

Some cellars may have the opposite problem—they need to be made more humid. (A cellar that is too dry will dry out corks and labels.) You can install a humidifier to remedy this, or, if you already have a cooler, make sure that it has a humidity control. Or you can use the classic methods: Have a sand floor that you water down periodically, and/or keep large, open water containers in the corners, which you refill as they evaporate.

Let There Be Light?

All light harms wine, even sunlight. A cellar should be kept in obscurity and should never see the light of day. The wine bottle itself serves as a natural protection, with its thick glass; still, overexposure can dry the cork, fade the labels, and tire the wine by making it age too rapidly. Any artificial light should be indirect, not too bright, and used as infrequently as possible.

Good Vibrations?

There is no such thing as a good vibration for a bottle of wine. Too much jostling and bustling will disturb the deposits that are trying to form, and will disrupt the maturation process. If you live over a subway station, truck depot, or construction site, you may have a problem. The best solution is to place your freestanding wine racks on shock absorbers, such as rubber pads. If you have stationary shelving, you can place layers of bubble wrap between the bottles. And be on the lookout for individual refrigeration units for your apartment. Just remember to avoid models whose motors turn on and off too violently, and therefore perpetually rattle your bottles.

Aeration

At the risk of contradicting myself, I will now point out that it is very important to have a flow of outside air, or ventilators, in your cellar. How do you do this while keeping the temperature constant? The honest answer: It's hard. Two little ventilators or basement windows, one up near the ceiling and one down near the floor, should do the trick. This will allow air to circulate yet avoid air currents. Try to place these ventilators low on the north side and high on the south side, or on the north and east sides, in order to escape the sun's rays at the hottest part of the day.

Aeration is important because it serves as a natural humidity control and air purifier, especially if you stock other perishables in your cellar, such as fruit and vegetables. The airing will keep your wine from absorbing the odors of any foodstuffs, humidity, dust, and so on, in your cellar.

ALTERNATIVES TO CELLARS

What do you do if you have a small collection of fifty to a hundred bottles of wine and don't want to make any major investments? You can adapt almost any corner of unused space in your apartment or home—a closet, a cupboard, a stairwell—to wine storage. It is important that the spot be dark, cool, and far from any vibrations. Keep the bottles away from electric appliances such as refrigerators, generators, heaters, and the like. One of the worst sites I ever saw for a wine rack was in my parents' home in Arizona. They have one of those enormous double-door, floor-to-ceiling, built-in refrigerator/freezers, and on top is a beautiful built-in wooden wine rack. But put a bottle of wine there and you expose it to the heat and vibrations of the refrigerator, the kitchen lights, and, even worse, the direct sunlight streaming in from the windows and skylights. Obviously, this is not a good idea! Kitchens, laundry rooms, porches, and similar spaces, are out.

A hall or bedroom closet, or, better yet, a big closet under a stairway (this is what I have) is a very good spot. Just get rid of your *National Geographic* collection, empty shoeboxes, and golf clubs, and make room for the more important things in life. Insulation made from polystyrene panels or mineral walling is sufficient to maintain the almost-constant temperature required for the correct storage of bottles. Nothing you couldn't put together over a weekend!

Temperature-Controlled Cabinets

One of the best wine-storage solutions for apartment dwellers and homeowners alike is the terribly smart and efficient indoor temperature-controlled storage units now on the market. These are about the size of a refrigerator—approximately twenty-seven inches wide by twenty-nine inches deep—and they can store some 250

SCENARIOS AND SOLUTIONS
FOR YOUR WINE STORAGE

Scenario #1:
Apartment, 50–500 bottles to store.

Solutions:
- Dry corner of the building's basement or common area.
- Cool, calm corner somewhere in apartment.
- Refrigerated wine storage cabinet.
- Rental space at wine store, or friend's basement or cellar.

Scenario #2:
Apartment, 500–2000+ bottles to store.
Solutions:
- Rental space at wine store.
- Converted room or large closet of the apartment.
- Small storage space or temperature-controlled wine cabinet in apartment for immediate access to early-drinking wine stock; rental space for wines needing long-term aging.
- Converted, built-in corner in building's basement: a cage-like metal wall in a corner or a cement block or brick wall.

Scenario #3:
Detached, individual house of recent architecture without a cellar, 500 to thousands of bottles to store.
Solutions:
- Dug-out, make-it-yourself cellar.
- Prefabricated cellar.
- Garage (only if well-insulated from temperature changes and odors).
- Very large temperature-controlled wine cabinet.

Scenario #4:
Large individual house with large cellar, many bottles to store.
Solution:
- A perfect wine cellar—storing conditions to make a Christie's rep proud, a security system to satisfy your insurer.

127

HOW TO CHOOSE
A TEMPERATURE-CONTROLLED CABINET

1. Determine how many bottles you have and how many you wish to eventually add.
2. Decide if you want to stock only those wines for aging, or if you prefer to keep some wines for aging (at cellar temperature) and others at service temperature.
3. Decide how you want to organize your collection. Will you have lots of bottles of the same cru or region? Or a few bottles of many different regions and styles?
4. Where do you want to place this cabinet?
5. What range of temperatures occurs in the place where you want to locate the cabinet? (Kitchen, office, garage . . .)
6. How much room do you have? In other words, what size cabinet can you accommodate?

All of these decisions will help you choose the right unit for your apartment or home.

bottles. You are guaranteed a constant temperature and ideal humidity at minimal cost. These very practical devices are even being taken up by restaurants and the châteaux themselves, so try them. The only drawbacks are that they can be expensive (though far less so than building a cellar!) and they are not practical for an extensive collection—five hundred or more bottles. Still, these are good storage solutions for an office, for an apartment, or for keeping those wines for consumption on hand if you are lucky enough to have the rest of your collection in an even larger cellar. Some models even offer the possibility to store wines at several temperatures; the coolest on the bottom for long-term, and a serving temperature on the top for current use.

Storage with a Local Wine Merchant

One of the easiest storage options is to leave your wine with a local wine merchant. You might be charged a storage or rental fee, depending upon the amount of wine you have and your relationship with the shop, but you will enjoy practically total quality control and security. Do inspect the merchant's storage facilities to verify that they are not interrupted by deliveries or frequent inventory checks that would cause conditions to fluctuate. Try to find a shop where long-term storage facilities are separate from stock facilities. Also, inquire about insurance coverage, and determine whether your storage fees include insurance for theft, fire, and flood.

If you store your wine collection with some merchants you might be obliged to purchase a certain amount of wine from them each year, since they are renting you space. Others might not care where you make your purchases. Many of the large, well-known wine merchants provide storage facilities in their shops for their most frequent and important clients, and thus might be more strict about what wines enter their shop.

The obvious disadvantage to this kind of arrangement is that you have access to your wines only when the shop is open: Planning and organization are required in order to have your wines when you need them. There will be no indulging spur-of-the-moment caprices. It thus makes sense to use this option for wines that have been put down for a number of years, keeping your more drinkable brews at home.

Installing a Ready-Made Cellar—or Building Your Own

These are rather drastic options—there's no way you'd

129

ever catch me digging a hole for five consecutive weekends! But they are possible. You can build either a traditional, stone cellar or "The Spiral Cellar," which is a cylindrical cellar invented by Georges Harnois in 1978. It is of premade modular concrete construction (it comes with steps and bottle racks), built into a pit, and lined to make it waterproof. This is an inexpensive alternative to building a cellar or converting an entire basement.

If you prefer to have someone do the work for you, contact a local contractor or landscape artist; they can steer you to an appropriate firm. More and more there are "cellar designers" cropping up—people who specialize in designing and constructing wine cellars according to your specifications. You can easily find one of these by contacting your chamber of commerce or a local architectural firm.

Keep in mind that your local climate is very important in choosing the best cellar for you. For example, in a state such as Arizona, temperature-controlled refrigeration units are practically the only choice. The rapid and drastic fluctuations in temperature of the desert climate are catastrophic for wines kept in any other type of cellar. The earth is so warm, the soil so special, that any fabricated cellar is unable to withstand the changes.

Colorado, on the other hand, has unusually dry air, and a cellar with a cool humidity of up to 70 percent is necessary. In Virginia, you might want to use a "ducted system"—the equivalent of central air-conditioning—to cool the cellar to a constant 57 degrees F. Be sure that there are several air-supply vents for better air distribution, and keep the humidity at between 60 and 75 percent.

If you live in Ohio, a cellar built by lowering your basement floor a foot and a half or so might keep your wine at a very cold 48 degrees F and 80 percent humidity, so that it can mature as slowly as possible. Battling

THE PREFABRICATED CELLAR

The Spiral Cellar
Georges Harnois's prefabricated concrete wine cellar can be installed under almost any home in a week. It comes with its own waterproof liner, which means it can be installed in areas with a high water table. The cellar is 2 meters wide and comes in depths of 2.00, 2.25, and 3.00 meters. It is entered via a trapdoor in the floor leading to a spiral staircase with a honeycomb of modules lining the walls. It holds up to 1600 bottles of wine and can be installed in garages, new extensions, or any room where there is a 2.50 meter diameter space to excavate.

The Mini Cellar
This is a small version of the Spiral Cellar, which comes in depths of 0.85, 1.10, and 1.35 meters. This has a simple wooden staircase leading from a double trapdoor. It's perfect for people who want to store 300 to 600 bottles and again can be installed anywhere in an existing home provided there is sufficient space.

Wine Hives
Wine hives were also developed in France from a special leca concrete. They have been designed to absorb vibration and humidity and to keep wines in the dark. They offer a cocoon for fine wines and will also help to control temperature. They come in two sizes, for 12 or 24 bottles. An attractive ochre color, they weigh over 40 pounds each and are reinforced so they can be stacked on top of each other without having to secure them to a wall. Perfect for garages, cellars, utility rooms, under stairwells, and in any other corner you can think of.

131

dryness in Nevada could be done with a sophisticated water-cooled ducted refrigeration system adjusted to keep things at 54 degrees F and 70 percent humidity.

In Maryland, a solution might be to lay a ten-inch-thick brick wall just inside the concrete shell of your basement. An Accutemp air-handling unit will keep the temperature at 55 degrees F, with 75 percent humidity. You could also vapor seal and insulate the room, because bricks are not exactly the greatest insulators.

And then there is Houston, where basements are practically unheard of because the water table is about eight feet. One wine-loving construction worker there placed sheet piling into the ground around the hole that was to become his cellar. Even that couldn't hold back the tides, however, and he ended up installing concrete, insulation, and a continuously pumped gravel drainage area in addition to the piling—and all of this merely to keep the waterlogged earthen walls from caving in! To top it off he installed double-pane thermal glass to prevent fogging, and doors with roller latches to avoid rusty locks and key-holes.[9] An admirable feat by a true wine lover. You see, there are as many solutions to cellar construction as there are problems and individual personalities.

HOW ARE YOU GOING TO ORGANIZE YOUR BOTTLES?

Finally, you've arrived at the fun part! How are you going to arrange all of your lovely specimens? There are an unlimited number of ways to organize a collection, none of them really right or wrong. If the majority of your wine comes from one particular region, you can organize the bottle into red wines, white wines, sweet wines, champagne or sparkling, fortified, and so on. Or you can

9. Ted Loos. "Great American Cellars," *Wine Spectator* (August 31, 1996): 58–92.

organize your wines by region: Bordeaux, Burgundy, Tuscany, Oregon. . . .

No matter which method you choose, however, be sure to place wines for longer aging on the bottom, and those wines meant for early consumption closer to the top—or at least in a more accessible spot. Or go a step further and store the rarest and oldest in a separate place entirely.

What to Organize Them In: Boxes, Cases, Shelves, and Whatnot

The easiest type of container to use in your cellar is the simple and classic wine rack. (Avoid storing wine bottles in their original crates or cartons.) Although metal racks are popular, I'd vote for racks made from wood or terra-cotta, which don't rattle the way metal ones do. As I've mentioned, store bottles horizontally, to keep their corks moist. Also, place the bottles with the label facing upward, so that deposits form on the lower backside of each bottle.

In addition to storing older bottles in the back or bottom, use tags or labels to help you identify individual bottles without having to touch and disturb them. You can also cover your most precious, oldest bottles in plastic bags to protect their labels from humidity.

The Paraphernalia

Second only to the ludic organizing of your bottles is the fun of equipping yourself with all of the necessary accessories: corkscrews, spittoons, glasses, *tastevins*, thermometers, decanters, the cellar registry book . . . not to mention all of the wine-related antiques you can collect and use for decoration (old wine presses, barriques, and so on). They

133

may be amusing, but these toys are also essential to monitoring your collection.

Monitoring and Managing Your Collection

As I have mentioned previously, the test case of wine is very important. As you're tracking the evolution of your wine, you'll want to open a bottle of each cru you're following perhaps every six months, when it's within three years of its approximate maturity date, and then a little more frequently within a year of this date. So why not set up a little tasting corner where you can invite a friend or two and have room to decant and take notes?

When you buy a particular wine, ask about its estimated date of maturation, or apogee. Remember the previous discussion about vintage charts (see page 43), and complement this with your own assessment. Another detail that should not be overlooked is the size of the bottle, because it can determine the time a wine takes to mature and therefore its value. A wine evolves more slowly in a magnum than in a bottle (750 milliliters), and correspondingly in a bottle than in a 500-milliliter half-bottle. The same wine always ages better in a magnum than a smaller bottle, although we don't know why. Some say it is simply the fact that, because of the volume of the bottle, the wine contacts the air more slowly, which slows down the maturation process. If you take a grand old bottle of red Burgundy that is nearly dead or dying, for example, and compare it to a magnum of the same wine and the same vintage, the Burgundy in the magnum may still be at its apogee, thus giving the magnum greater value for the same volume. So try to purchase wines intended for long cellaring in larger bottles. Here is the size range of Bordeaux bottles:

Magnum:	1.5 liters or 2 bottles
Marie-Jeanne:	2.5 liters or more than 3 bottles
Double Magnum:	3 liters or 4 bottles
Dame-Jeanne:	4 liters or more than 5 bottles
Jeroboam:	4.5 liters or 6 bottles
Impériale:	6 liters or 8 bottles

The Cellar Book

Today the market is flooded with computer software that can organize your bottles, provide tasting commentaries and a place for your own comments, dictate your bottles' maturation dates and keep track of which have been removed from the cellar. Very handy, but hardly necessary for the average collector—who has fewer than five hundred bottles! Human-size cellars can still be handled by a simple *livre de cave,* or "cellar book." The painstaking entry of each beloved purchase is an integral part of the ceremony and tradition of collecting. Don't deprive yourself of it.

There are hundreds of variations on the cellar book available. It can be decorative, adding a look of authenticity and charm to your cellar, or commemorative, recording all of those wonderful moments when bottles are opened and shared. But its most important role is a practical one. It ensures that you know what wines you have at all times; that each one is opened at the right time; and that your collection is not wasted and drunk too late.

The choice of a cellar book is a personal one; you'll need to find the format that best suits your wine style, buying patterns, and drinking habits. My advice is to create one of your own on a computer, print it on lovely parchment paper, and have it bound. My personal cellar book has a place for each entry's purchase information,

135

Wine:

Producer:

Address:

Tel: Fax:

Date bought: Price:

Tasting notes and dates:

Location in cellar

Vintage

Quantity

To Drink from

To drink young

To age

18°C
16°C
14°C
12°C
10°C
8°C
6°C

OPTIMAL SERVING TEMPERATURE

136

137

Wine:

Producer:

Address:

Tel: Fax:

Date bought: Price:

Tasting notes and dates:

_____

_____

_____

_____

Location in cellar	
To Drink from	
Quantity	
Vintage	

OPTIMAL SERVING TEMPERATURE

18°C
16°C
14°C
12°C
10°C
8°C
6°C

To drink young

To age

technical data (grape varieties, yields, vinification details), and speculated rate of maturation, as well as a place to glue in the label if I like. Of course there is also plenty of room to note when I opened the bottle, with whom and where I drank it, what was eaten with it, and my impressions. It has become more a scrapbook or diary than anything else—so much so that I couldn't dare let anyone read it!

A basic book should allow you to record the following essentials: the name of the wine, the region of production, the vintage, the producer's name, the place you acquired it, the date you acquired it, the price, the quantity acquired, and the size of the bottles. There should also be an "add and subtract" column that reflects your consumption and purchases. I've included an example of a registry page. You can make photocopies, or use it as a model to create your own. For it is difficult to find a premade system that takes into account your personal taste, your cellar size, your organization, and your preferred fashion of caring for and following your wines.

With the proper storage conditions and the right tools, you have everything you need to nurture your collection. Remember that all there really is to monitoring it correctly is tasting the wine frequently! Make allowances for personal taste and human error, and you should be fine.

SERVING AND TASTING

"Wine is the intellectual part of the meal."
—Alexandre Dumas

he long-awaited moment. You've been eying that Richebourg for months . . . years. You've plotted its evolution meticulously in your registry. You've counted the days. You've even planned the menu for this soon-to-be historic event. Now you've decided that it's time.

There are a lot of misconceptions about serving wine. All too frequent is the image of a tuxedo-clad waiter deftly wielding candles, decanters, and other paraphernalia. What is he doing? It all seems very dramatic, and yet there is a simple logic behind all of this mystery. Remember that for every rule there is an exception, and that every rule must defer to personal taste.

THE RIGHT ENVIRONMENT

How important are your surroundings when you prepare to drink a bottle of wine? Very. A bottle of simple red wine from Provence might not carry it off in the elegant salon of a three-star restaurant (even if married with Provençal cooking), but it will steal the show when served with the same meal in a more casual, less ornate setting. Can't explain it but it's true. There are banquet wines and there are barbecue wines.

There is also a "correct" way to serve wines if you wish to stand on ceremony. These "rules" concern having the right stemware, table setting, and wine temperature, then "testing," decanting, and serving the wine in the correct order. These rites may appear silly, but they can truly add to the pleasure of a wine.

THE RIGHT ACCESSORIES

The right glass does make a difference. Drinking lovely old Bordeaux in a plastic beach tumbler detracts from its allure. And even aside from its aesthetic advantages, there is the more important point that glass is the best material for containing wine and exhibiting its qualities. Clear, well-formed glasses allow us a better visual inspection, a step essential to wine tasting. If you want to get very fancy, there exists a wineglass shape for every region and type of wine: Alsace, Bordeaux, Bourgogne, sherry, Champagne, and so on. I prefer a classic all-purpose form from the "Oenologue" series, a standard wine-tasting model, for all wines except Cognac, sherry, and Champagne (which have their own more appropriate vessels). They are pretty, practical, delicate enough to dress a formal table yet casual enough for daily brew, and sturdy enough for the dishwasher. Champagne should always be drunk from tulip-shaped glasses rather than the Helen of Troy breast-mold version, which was popular in the 1950s and 1960s but abandoned because they let all of the gases escape.

SMOKING

Now this is a chapter in itself. I used to be a militant nonsmoker, and I guess I still am where cigarettes are concerned. But once I started wine tasting professionally, I found myself surrounded by cigar smokers, and quickly learned to appreciate this art. Still, smoking, whether it be a cigarette or a cigar, is meant for *after* the wine in most situations, and certainly at a professional tasting or formal event. Even at home, I ask guests not to not smoke between courses but to wait for the dessert, coffee, and Cognac. This is generally the accepted rule.

WHO TESTS THE WINE?

This is a rather new etiquette problem. When at home, it is the host or hostess who is in charge of the wine who first tests it, subsequently serving it to the first guest on the right. Tradition says that the male host should serve it to the lady on his right, then counterclockwise to all of the ladies, and finally returning around the table clockwise to all of the men. If the hostess is taking care of the wine, then she should follow the same counterclockwise rule. It's up to you to decide if service should be ladies-first. More and more wine is simply served in the most convenient order.

In restaurants, wine waiters often automatically ask the man who ordered the food to taste the wine, even if someone else made the wine order.

In my opinion, wine service should not be a sex issue. It is an issue of logic. The person who is designated the wine selector (if not the host or hostess) by fellow diners should be the taster, unless organized otherwise. Serving note: It is a good idea to smell the inside of your glass before serving. Sometimes residue soap or dust can interfere with the wine. Also, remember to never fill the glass entirely. Use big glasses and fill only one third to one half. This allows the wine to continue airing and leaves room for swirling.

WHAT IS THE RIGHT TEMPERATURE?

The most common mistake concerning service temperature is that moderation is ignored. Wines are almost always served too chilled or too warm. Colder temperatures paralyze the taste buds on our tongues, and we lose the fruit and aromas of the wine. Wines that are served too chilled thus have no aroma, no chance to develop. This is why often restaurants serve a poor-quality wine straight from the refrigerator: It's so cold you don't notice that it was a cheap wine from the start. Why do you think that Beaujolais Nouveau is served so chilled?

The same thing happens when a wine is served too warm. The greatest misconception concerning wine temperature is that all great reds need to be served *chambré*, or at room temperature. This practice was established, however, when central heating did not exist, and the average temperature of a room in a stone house or château was much cooler than in a modern dwelling. There is nothing worse than a too-warm Pinot Noir; it becomes overly alcoholic, heavy, and boring. A Burgundy should be served several degrees cooler than a Bordeaux, thus preserving its fruit and personality. And unlike a chilled wine, an overheated wine is usually lost. It has become oxidized and cannot be brought back to life. The older the wine, the truer this is.

SERVING TEMPERATURES

SPARKLING WINES
Simple sparkling 39–45° F
(Cavas, Crémant, Saumur, nonvintage champagne)
Sweet sparkling 39–45° F
Finest sparkling and vintage champagne 43–46° F

WHITE WINES
Simple, sweet white wines (Anjou Blanc, Muscats, German
    QbAs) 43–46° F
Simple, crisp, dry whites (Muscadet, Sancerre, Sauvignon
    Blancs, Pinot Blanc) 43–46° F
Complex dry whites (Burgundy, Graves, Rioja) 48–52° F
Medium-sweet whites (German Spätlese, Auslese, New World
    Rieslings) 50–54° F
Finest sweet whites
(Classed-growth Sauternes, top German wines, late-harvest
    wines) 52–55° F
Finest dry whites
(Mature white Burgundies, Graves, top New World
    Chardonnays) 50–54° F

ROSÉ WINES
Simplest should be most chilled 43–46° F

RED WINES
Early-drinking reds (Loire, simple Beaujolais, Côtes du Rhône,
    vins de pays) 50–54° F
Simple red wines (young Bordeaux and Burgundies, New
    World reds) 57–59° F
Complex, mature reds, notably Pinot Noirs (Burgundies, New
    World Pinot Noirs, Italian and Spanish reds) 61–63° F

143

Mature fine red wines, notably Cabernet Sauvignons
(Classed-growth Bordeaux, serious New World
Cabernets, Rhônes) 61–63° F

FORTIFIED WINES
Dry (Fino sherries) 48–52° F
Medium (Amontillado sherries, Madeiras, white ports) 50–54° F
Sweet (cream sherries, tawny ports, vintage ports) 59–61° F

HOW TO CHILL A WINE

You shouldn't need to chill a wine if you keep your *cave* at
the correct temperature. Still, chilling is handy to know if
you've bought a bottle or been offered one that has not
been stored correctly. There are three ways to do it: Put
the bottle in an ice bucket, run cool tap water over it, or
put it in the refrigerator. This last method is perceived as
being the most likely to shock the bottle—but this is
untrue as long as the wine is not left too long, and you
avoid the freezer. Remember that a wine dies at 27
degrees F.

HOW TO BRING A WINE TO "ROOM TEMPERATURE"

This process is a little more complicated and delicate. It is
meant to bring a wine out of its hibernation, or storage
period. The French word *chambré* is the adjective form of
the word *chambre*, or "room"; in the past, wines were
brought to the correct temperature in dining rooms, which
were then kept at 61 to 64 degrees F, maximum. Don't
make the abominable mistake of leaving a wine in a 68- or
73-degree room, and if you do, don't leave it for long.

If your *cave* is not very cold, heating your wineglass between your hands will suffice. There is no point in putting a bottle on a source of warmth, such as a heater or radiator, or in boiling water. Prerinsing a carafe with hot water so that the heat passes from the glass to the wine, though, is acceptable.

What is most important in warming a wine—more so than when you are chilling one—is to make sure that there is not an enormous difference between the temperature of the *cave* and that of the room.

How to Serve Different Wines at the Same Meal

- Chilled wines come before room-temperature wines.
- Younger wines come before older ones.
- Lighter wines come before heavier, coarser ones.
- White wines come before red.
- Red wines come before sweet white wines (unless the sweet white has been served as an apéritif or with a first course, such as foie gras).

Wines served from the same wine region should be served in reverse order of vintage, the younger before the older, even if the younger is a better growth—though, there may, of course, be exceptions to this. The idea is to save the heavier, more complex wines for last so as to not spoil the palate for the lighter wines.

How to Open a Bottle

I've drunk enough wine with cork particles in it to take this process seriously. First, you need the right corkscrew. My favorites are the Screwpull and the "butterfly" styles. I prefer the screwpull, because it requires no physical effort whatsoever. Even better, use the Screwpull's "foil cutter" first (new on the market is a Screwpull with a built-in foil cutter), to neatly and cleanly cut off the metal capsule; the whole operation then takes sixty seconds. (I know, I timed it. I was thirsty.) Very old bottles may have wax capsules, which should be chipped off. Essential is not to massacre the cork, which, especially in old bottles, can be very fragile. It is also important to eliminate enough of the metal capsule so that the wine does not come into contact with it while you pour; this can give the wine a bad taste. Next, clean off the interior and exterior of the rim, to get rid of any last bits of cork or foil. Usually the host or designated bottle opener will want to "pour" the cork. By pouring a drop or two into the glass, you can quickly verify that the wine is not spoiled, and can also avoid having any errant cork crumbs fall into a guest's glass.

146

Opening a Champagne Bottle

Opening a bottle of Champagne can be very tricky . . . and very dangerous. Letting the cork pop off with a joyful explosion is the worst thing you can do to the Champagne (and sometimes to your health). Instead, remove the foil from the top of the bottle and place your hand on top of the cork, covering it. Do not remove your hand until the cork is off, no matter how cumbersome this posture becomes. Then take off the wire, or loosen it completely, with your other hand. Wrap a towel around the bottle to avoid its slipping and leaking. Next remove the cork gently by slowly turning the bottle in one direction and the cork in the other. Ease the bottle open, don't yank it. You want to almost push the cork back into the bottle, resisting the pressure, until you hear a soft, hissing sigh, not a "pop." When you pop a cork open, the carbon dioxide gas escapes—and there go your bubbles.

If you have forgotten to chill your Champagne and the guests are hammering on the door, don't put it in the freezer—it can explode within twenty minutes. A better idea is to put it in an ice-filled bucket. You'll have it ready to drink in ten to fifteen minutes.

And again, always serve your Champagne in narrow, small-rimmed glasses. This helps it keep its bubbles longer.

Cork Sniffing

You've seen people smell the cork after opening a bottle. Do they really need to do that? And why is it done? Most amateurs would reply that they are testing the quality of the wine. The main thing a cork can tell you about a wine is whether or not it is *bouchonné*, or corked, which means that the cork has developed mold that has penetrated it and tainted the wine.

What is also worth doing is looking at the cork for leakage: If the cork is soaked with liquid up through to the top, there may have been leakage, and your wine may be oxidized or spoiled. White crystals on the bottom of the cork are simply tartar, which is quite normal in white wines stored at cold temperatures.

What else should you check? The wine's origin. An original cork will have the vintage and château printed on it. If it doesn't, it may mean that the bottle is a fraud or, in the case of a very old vintage, that it has been recorked. If the recorking was not done at the château of origin and the cork re-marked, then the bottle has lost its authenticity as far as resale value is concerned, because you are no longer able to guarantee its identity.

147

When Should You Uncork?

If you think you're properly airing a bottle by uncorking it and letting it sit a while, you've missed the point. Most wines do not need airing; once they are at drinking temperature, they can immediately be poured into a carafe and served.

TO DECANT OR NOT TO DECANT

Decanting is done for two reasons: to separate wine from any sediment that may have formed in the bottle, and to allow contact with the air, which should help accelerate the wine's maturation. The general rule is that old wines are decanted to remove their sediment, and young ones, to help open them up. But most wines don't need decanting; they can be served directly from the bottle. That being said, you can't hurt a wine by decanting it, except perhaps a very old, fragile wine that would become bruised or would disappear if exposed to the air for too long. Decanting used to be required, because of past winemaking methods, but given modern techniques (stabilizing, fining, and so on) it is only the older—but not oldest—wines with deposits that need such treatment.

There are several pros and cons to decanting. The essential determinants of your choice should be the age of the wine and the length of time you will leave it to decant. Proponents believe that decanting even the youngest wines for a couple of hours permits them to soften and round up a bit. But the risk is that too long a decanting will rob a wine, even a young one, of its vitality and freshness. For example, a tannic red Bordeaux five years old could withstand only several hours of decanting. An older wine can regain its freshness by decanting,

148

but could lose some aroma if it's left too long. So the key is to go ahead and decant whatever you like—but not for long, never more than an hour. Even mature white wines can't be hurt by a little aeration—but to be sure, do so just before serving. You can't go wrong by always betting on the modest side: Don't forget, aeration continues when the wine is poured into the glass and again when it's swirled about in the glass. Add this time to your decanting calculations.

Decanting itself is a far easier procedure than is believed. The essential first step is to verify that the decanter and the glasses are clean. Musty odors from cardboard storage boxes or soapy films from dishwashing liquid can kill a wine. A professional taster will always smell the glass first to check for any impurities. Before decanting an older wine, you can rinse the carafe with warm water, which warms the glass of the carafe and, in turn, the wine. Decanting a young wine is easy: Just pour it into a clean vessel and let it stand for an hour or so, uncovered, while surveying its temperature. If you wish to serve it fresh, let it decant in a cool area—not, for example, in the kitchen while you prepare the roast.

Decanting older wines requires a little more attention. It is best to work against a white background (such as a tablecloth) and/or with a candle lit behind the bottle, so as to better observe the wine's deposits. Either with or without a funnel, gently and slowly pour the wine into the decanter. Keeping the stream steady is very important; this will ensure that the sediment is not disturbed. If used, the candle should illuminate the neck of the bottle, so that when you near the end of the bottle you can watch closely for the first signs of deposit—a black, cloudy sediment—to enter the neck of the bottle. Stop pouring at this point. Put the stopper in the decanter and,

149

if you like, give the decanter a few large swirls to aerate the wine (this shouldn't bruise it).

Let a very old wine sit in the decanter before serving, covered with the stopper. This will prevent it from fading. Older bottles should be stood up a day before serving, to give the deposits a chance to sink to the bottom. Using a cradle or a basket is an easy way to keep the deposits localized on the lower side of the bottle while you uncork it.

Which Wines Can Be Decanted?

RED WINES LIKELY TO HAVE DEPOSITS
Top Bordeaux crus five or more years old
Top Burgundy crus ten or more years old
Some of the top Rhônes of five or more years
Italian Barolos of five or more years
Older Spanish Penedès of seven or more years
Vintage ports
Cabernets Sauvignons, Shiraz, and Pinot Noirs from
    California, Australia, or Chile of seven or more years

YOUNGER RED WINES TO DECANT
Younger Bordeaux, crus bourgeois, and petits châteaux
Young Burgundy crus, most Beaujolais, village wines
Rhône wines younger than five years
Provençal, Midi, and Loire reds
Most quality red wines from other countries

THE OCCASIONAL WHITES TO DECANT
Old Loire wines, older Graves, vendange tardive from Alsace
German Rhein and Mosel wines of ten or more years
Mature Spanish Riojas

NOT TO DECANT

Really old Burgundies and Bordeaux should not be decanted but simply stood up twenty-four to forty-eight hours before serving: Decanting them would risk damaging them. Likewise mature white wines, such as a Meursault from Burgundy, for the same reason. Then, of course, you don't need to decant young white wines, and you *shouldn't* decant sparkling wines and Champagne.

HOW TO TASTE WINE

Why do we taste wines? What are we looking for? The answer is balance—among the acids, tannins, alcohol, and fruit. Acids give the backbone, tannins the preservation and longevity, alcohol the structure, and fruit the taste. The better made a wine is, the more balanced it will be, and the longer it will last.

Tasting wine can be hard work. Really. It's easy to take the act of tasting for granted: We all taste every day, all day long. What is so difficult? It's having to break down the different components of taste and then analyze them. Anyone can do it, but it takes concentration and practice. The more you taste, the more "memory" you have, and the more you receive information with which to create your own standards. There are all kinds of exercises you can use to learn to differentiate wines. As your skill increases these exercises will take you from being able to blindly taste the difference between a red and white wine; to recognizing a Cabernet Sauvignon from a Pinot Noir grape; to discerning whether the grape was grown in France, the United States, or Australia; to determining if the wine was made in a hot or cool climate; to being able to tell a young wine from an older one.

151

In the beginning you should do comparative tastings, comparing wines from the same appellation, or vintage, or grape variety. Always find a common theme to help you start establishing tasting patterns; this also helps you recognize, describe, and discriminate among the wines. It is only the advanced or professional taster who can identify a wine on its own, and this is because the notes required to recognize or analyze it are filed away in the taster's memory. Your own goal as you learn how to taste a wine should be to determine its quality, or whether or not it is well made. So, here goes.

The tasting of a wine is basically broken into three processes: Sight, Smell, and Taste.

Sight

- Holding your glass vertically, look down upon it from directly above. This will allow you to view the wine's surface, clearness, and depth of color, along with any CO_2 (bubbles) that may be present.
- With the glass tilted almost horizontally against a white tablecloth, look at the wine at its center as well as its "rim." The center, or "eye," of the wine will reveal its hue, and help you know its age. The lighter, or rubier red, a red wine is, the younger it is. Once it takes on redbrick or orange tones, you know it is older. By looking at its rim, you can also determine its age. The younger the wine the thinner the watery rim will be; the older the wine, the thicker.
- Now look at the wine horizontally with your eyes directly at its "disk" level. The disk is the uppermost level of the wine. This helps you determine both age and clarity.
- Tilt the glass so that a little wine covers its sides (a

glass should never be filled more than one-third when tasting; at the table, never more than halfway). Look again at it horizontally at eye level this time, but watch the little "tears" or "legs" that are running down the sides. Are they slow and languorous or thin and rapid? The slower the legs run, the more glucose (sugar) is present in the wine; the more watery or quickly the legs run, the more alcohol is present. This will give you your first idea of how the wine may taste.

Smell

- Without swirling, smell the wine. This will permit you to pick up any varietal qualities or characteristics, along with secondary aromas (for Burgundies).
- Now swirl the glass and smell again. Use either one or both nostrils. It sounds odd, but experiment with each nostril—you might be surprised at the differences. My right nostril seems to be more accurate and sensitive than my left! You should be looking for

153

THE DIFFERENCE BETWEEN AROMA AND BOUQUET

Aromas are usually associated with the smell of the grape variety itself, and are most obvious while a wine is young. *Bouquet* refers to the complexity and development of aromas once a wine is matured or, more specifically, oak aged. An aroma is going to be fresh, vigorous, and spicy, whereas a bouquet is going to be sophisticated, subtle, and complex. In describing Burgundy, however, it's traditional to use the word *aroma* only. Aromas from the grape are then "primary" aromas, those from fermentation and oak aging are "secondary," and those developed during bottle aging are "tertiary."

major faults, and remarking any differences in aroma from when the wine was still. Here you'll find intense tertiary aromas (for young Burgundies) and a bouquet (for mature wines).

- If you think you've detected a fault, or if you can't seem to "wake up" the wine's nose, continue swirling, or cover the glass and shake it violently once or twice. This is an extreme measure, however, and rarely necessary.

Taste

154

- At this point, some people advise taking a small sip of wine. I tend to take large mouthfuls, which helps me to feel or "chew" the wine more easily. Or I take a small first sip and go through my analysis, then take a second, much larger sip and rinse it through my mouth like mouthwash to either confirm or discount my first impressions. It's up to you to decide what works best. This first taste is meant to determine the wine's *première bouche*, or "first attack." Is it soft or firm, smooth or sharp? How soon afterward do you feel the tannins, the acids, the "mouth"?

HOW WE TASTE

Very sensitive, but not specific

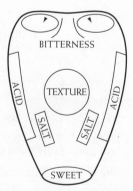

- Swish the wine around in your mouth. Go ahead and make that gurgling, airy noise between your teeth to aerate the wine. Swallow a tiny little bit. Concentrate on what is happening on your tongue and the sides of your mouth. Are you experiencing a puckering, drying sensation? (Young, tannic wines will do this.) Is it velvety smooth, with softened tannins (an older wine, correctly aged)? Is it like butter, all creamy and almost thick? This is where you can judge the wine's mouth. Is it ample or thin? Here, too, you can fully analyze the wine's flavors, intensity, and texture.

- Spit out the wine, breathe out through your nose and palate, and concentrate on the back of your mouth. Here you are analyzing the "finale," or finish of the wine. The better the wine, the longer it will linger in the back of your palate. Here also the balance among the tastes and aromas is important. A wine that has a delicious, up-front, and fruity attack, along with an ample and warm mouth, may disappoint once it gets to the finish. An overly alcoholic wine with lots of heavy fruit, spice, and oak flavors up front can fool you up until the finish; if this is short (or even nonexistent) you can be sure that the wine is unbalanced and has little chance of cellaring for very long.

155

WHAT DO
WINES TASTE LIKE?

White wine grape varieties generally smell and taste like citrus and other tree fruit, such as lemon, orange, grapefruit, and apple. In mature white wines, or sweet white wines, are reminders of pineapple, mango, apricot, pear, melon, and lychee.

> **Red wine grape** varieties generally taste like the red fruit
> family: black and red cherry, red and black currant, rasp-
> berry, strawberry, and plum.
>
> **Both red and white wines** can have odors and tastes such as
> mineral, spice, herbs, tobacco, hay, yeast, honey, caramel,
> and nuts. The tastes come from either the "terroir," or soil,
> the grape variety, the yeasts (if indigenous yeasts are not
> used to start fermentation), the fermentation period, or the
> oak for aging.

SERVING WINE AND FOOD

This is a vast topic that need not be developed here, but
it cannot be ignored, either—so I will be brief. There is
much ado today about food and wine pairings and about
"food wines"—those easily matched to strong foods. This
is a good and a bad thing. It is true that to persuade consumers to consider wine an everyday beverage essential to
a healthful diet, it had to be associated with food. Well
indeed does European culture teach us this. Unfortunately, these marketing efforts have gone almost too far;
consumers these days expect no more from a wine than
that it go well with their fettucine Alfredo and not overshadow their BBQ sparerib sauce.

But maybe we're overlooking the wine's personality?
Some wine producers have gone so far as to deliberately
make easy, light, noncommittal wines, precisely because
they are marketable, are consumer friendly, and get the
job done. These are probably not wines you would want
to put in your cellar, though.

At the same time, remember this: Which do you
choose first when planning a dinner, the wine or the main
course?

156

Another thought about food and wine pairings: You can break all of the rules. Remember being told that only white wine goes with fish, only red wine with red meat? It's not always true. Light, fruity red wines go very well with some fish; and heavy, mature white wines can take poultry and some game. It depends upon the sauce as much as the main ingredient. Lamb, for instance, can be served with a curry, mint, or red wine sauce, and all three versions of the same meat would take a different wine. And forget about sweet white wines being only for dessert. They can be served as an apéritif, with a first course of foie gras or quiche, with a main course of roast pork stuffed with prunes and apricots or chestnuts, and with a fruit salad or a green salad that has walnuts. They're also sublime with a platter of cheeses, especially blue cheese, Roquefort, mild and strong goat (but not the creamy sweet kind), Epoisses, and Beaufort. And all of this comes before you even *get* to dessert!

157

Another surprise is Champagne. People forget that Champagne is a wine and can take a meal from beginning to end. Champagne is issued from either the Chardonnay, Pinot Noir, or Pinot Meunier grape variety, giving it innumerable nuances. And other countries' sparkling wines also are issued from a variety of grapes, each with its own character and flavor. I often start an evening by serving a light, lemony blanc de blancs as an apéritif; bring that into the first course of foie gras on toasted brioche or Coquilles St. Jacques with a Champagne, mushroom, and cream sauce (the Champagne is much better with foie gras than the traditional Sauternes because it seems to cut through the fat and underline the dish's delicate perfumes); Drink a vintage rosé or a full-bodied blanc de noirs with a lamb roast; serve a nutty, toasty blanc de noirs with a salad of mâche (lamb's lettuce), Roquefort, and walnuts in a walnut-oil dressing; and end with a fruity demi-sec for the chocolate mousse. Nothing beats ending a meal on Champagne; it is light and digestible. So break all of the rules and create taste combinations for yourself. The only essential is that both the wine's and the food's personality is respected and complemented, and that neither one is dominated. Remember, food is meant to complement wines just as much as, or even more than wine is meant to complement the food. If a wine brings forward an aspect of the food, and the food reinforces an element of the wine, then a successful match has been made. If only matchmaking for humans was so easy!

158

HOW TO DETECT WINE FAULTS

Oxidized wines (excess contact with oxygen): White wines will have a dull, flat appearance and will be darker than they should for their age—almost a rust or brown color. They will have a flat, stale nose and a sharp (overcooked) taste. They'll remind you of Madeira, and are therefore also referred to as "madeirized" wines. Red wines will also be dull and brown and will taste like burned caramel.

Volatile wines are those that taste like vinegar from their volatile, or acetic, acid. They can even smell like nail polish remover; they're thin in texture and sharp and sour in taste.

Wines containing **sulfur dioxide** will have a pungent, acrid smell, like that of a match being lit. On the mouth they will be dry and prickling.

Wines with **hydrogen sulfide** will smell of bad eggs or of a combination of rubber, garlic, and rotted vegetables. They will also taste that way.

A Basic Tasting Vocabulary

A lot of hullaballo is often made about wine-tasting terms. While it's true that some people get carried away, it's also kind of fun to get wrapped up in a game of metaphors, hyperbole, personification, and imagery with like-minded wine neurotics. More important, the basic tasting vocabulary, if used, allows wine lovers from all over the world to speak together with a little cohesion and homogeneity. If we all taste the same thing in a wine and call it twenty different things, or if we all have our own interpretation of the same word, we'll never get anywhere. Plus, having an established vocabulary helps us relate a wine's smell or taste to something similar. The words themselves actually stimulate our own impressions.

There are nine basic categories, or families, of smells:

1. **Floral**: rose, violet, acacia, jasmine, orange blossom, violet, lavender . . .

2. **Fruity**: red fruits/berries, cherry, plum, peach, apricot, orange, lemon, melon, grapefruit, pineapple, lychee, raspberry, apple . . .

3. **Spicy**: pepper, clove, licorice, anise, cinnamon, nutmeg, mint . . .

4. **Animal**: game, musk, horse, leather, damp fur, wet wool, cat's pee . . .

5. **Vegetal**: straw/hay, moss/undergrowth, grass, green pepper, tea, asparagus, olive, mushroom . . .

6. **Mineral**: chalky, volcanic, earthy, oily/petroleumlike . . .

7. **Chemical**: yeast, sulfur, ethyl acetate (nail polish), mercaptan (garlic), plastic . . .

8. **Empyreumatic**: burnt smells, tar, tobacco, coffee, smoke, caramel . . .

9. **Balsamic/Woody**: pine, oak, cedar, vanilla, turpentine . . .

For more wine-tasting terms, refer to the glossary.

159

APPENDIX: WINE AGENCIES, INSTITUTES, AND GOVERNMENTAL ORGANIZATIONS

Australian Wine Bureau
Wine Trade Director
630 Fifth Avenue, Suite 420
New York, NY 10100
Tel.: 212-408-8460
Fax: 212-265-2768

Berry Bros. & Rudd Ltd.
    Beverage
3 St. James's Street
London, SW1A 1EG
Tel.: 0171-396-9666
Fax: 0171-396-9611

Bordeaux Wine Bureau
c/o Food and Wines from France
215 Park Avenue South, Suite
    1601
New York, NY 10003
Tel.: 1-212-477-8492
Fax: 1-212-473-4315

CIV Importers
10419 Old Placerville Road
Suite 252
Sacramento, CA 95827
Dir: Vince Friend
Tel: 916-368-7188
Fax: 916-368-8932

Department of the Treasury
Office of Field Operations
Bureau of Alcohol, Tobacco and
    Firearms
Trade Compliance Division
New York, NY 10048-0951
Tel.: 212-927-0771
Fax: 212-927-0097

Entreprises de Grands Vins
    de France
95, rue de Monceau
75008 Paris

Tel.: 45-22-75-73
Fax: 45-22-94-16

German Wine Institute
Gutenbergplatz 3-5
6500 Mainz
Federal Republic of Germany

Hungarian Embassy
Commercial Councilor
Washington, D.C.
Tel.: 202-362-6730

Institut National des
    Appellations d'Origins
138, avenue des Champs-Elysées
45008 Paris
Tel.: 45-62-54-75
Fax: 42-25-57-97

International Wine Accessories
11020 Audelia Road, Suite B-113
Dallas, TX 75243
Tel.: 214-349-6097

Italian Trade Center
499 Park Avenue
New York, NY 10022
Tel.: 212-980-1500
Fax: 212-758-1050

Justerini & Brooks Ltd.
Wine Merchants Estd. 1749
61 St. James's Street
London, SW1A 1LZ
Tel.: 0171-493-8721
Fax: 0171-499-4653

Le Creuset of America, Inc.
P.O. Box 575

River Road
Yamassee, SC 29945
Tel.: 803-589-6211
Fax: 803-589-8106

National Association of
    Importers, Inc.
1025 Vermont Avenue NW,
    Suite 1066
Washington, DC 20005
Tel.: 202-638-1617
Fax: 202-638-3122

New York State Wine and
    Grape Foundation
350 Elm Street
Penn Yan, New York 14527
James Trezise
Tel.: 315-536-7442
Fax: 315-536-0719

Portuguese Trade Commission
Information Center
590 Fifth Avenue, 3rd Floor
New York, NY 10036-4702
Tel.: 212-354-4658
Fax: 212-575-4737

Rieja Wine
Sherry Institute of Spain
Wines from Spain
Lexington Avenue, Floors 44-45
New York, NY 10174-03331
Tel.: 212-661-4959
Fax: 212-972-2494

Sopexa (Food and Wine from
    France)
215 Park Avenue South
New York, NY 10003

Tel.: 212-477-9800
Fax: 212-473-4315

Syndicat des Coteaux du
    Languedoc
Mas Saporta
B.P. 9
34972 Lattes Cédex, France
Tel.: 67-92-20-70
Fax: 65-58-05-15

Syndicat des Vignerons
Récoltants d'Alsace
75008 Paris, France
Tel.: 44-94-80-80
Fax: 42-66-90-63
B.P. 1541
68015 Colmar, Alsace, France
Tel.: 89-41-97-41
Fax: 89-23-01-97

Syndicat du Cru Corbières
B.P. 111
11200 Lezignan-Corbières,
    France
Tel.: 68-27-04-34
Fax: 68-27-31-66

Syndicat Viticole de Sauternes
13, place de la Mairie
33210 Sauternes, France
Tel.: 56-63-24-76

Syndicat Viticole Régional des
    A.O.C. Bordeaux, Bordeaux
    Supérieur et Crémant de
    Bordeaux
Maison de la Qualité
33750 Beychac et Caillau,
    France

Tel.: 65-72-90-99
Fax: 56-72-81-02

Union des Grands Crus de
    Bordeaux
10, cours du XXX Juillet
33000 Bordeaux, France
Tel.: 56-51-91-91
Fax: 56-51-64-12

Union des Maisons de
    Champagne
1, rue Marie-Stuart
51100 Reims, France
Tel.: 26-47-90-58

Wine Enthusiast Companies
P.O. Box 392
Pleasantville, NY 10570-0392
Tel.: 914-789-8912
Fax: 914-789-8903

Wine Institute
c/o Research and Education
    Department
425 Market Street, Suite 1000
San Francisco, CA 94105
Tel.: 415-512-0151

Wine Institute of
    New Zealand, Inc.
Exports Manager
P.O. Box 90276
Auckland Meal Center
Auckland, New Zealand
Tel.: 00649-303-3527
Fax: 00649-302-2969

GLOSSARY OF
INTERNATIONAL WINE TERMS

ACID, ACETIC—An acid found in all wine, though usually in tiny quantities; excess amounts cause wine to turn to vinegar.

ACID, ASCORBIC—An acid with an antioxidizing effect that is often added to wine just before bottling. It is only effective in the presence of *sulfur dioxide.*

ACID, CITRIC—An acid present especially in citrus fruit, but also in lesser quantities in the grape. White grapes, particularly those affected by *noble rot,* contain more of it than red grapes do. As an additive, it is strictly controlled by law.

ACID, LACTIC—An acid that appears during the malolactic fermentation of wine, when *malic acid* changes into carbon dioxide and lactic acid. Eventually this fades and becomes imperceptible in tasting.

ACID, MALIC—Once the grape ripens, its malic acid (which is present at high levels in green grapes) decreases. Its tart taste of green apples makes this acid easily recognizable. The hotter the year, the faster it decreases during the ripening process, which is why it is more apparent when the weather has been colder.

ACID, TARTARIC—Regarded as the most "noble" acid. This has more acidifying power than any other acid contained in wine, and is not commonly found in other fruits. The tartaric acid content goes down as the grape ripens, then varies depending on the weather.

ACIDITY, FIXED—The total of all acids contained in the fruit itself, including tartaric, malic, lactic, and so on.

ACIDITY, REAL—The intensity of acidity, usually expressed as *pH* (potential hydrogen) on a scale of 0 to 14, with 7 representing total neutrality; 0 total acidity; and 14 total alkalinity. The usual pH of wine varies from around 3 to 4 on this scale.

ACIDITY, TOTAL—The combined total of *volatile acidity* and *fixed acidity*. This naturally varies, depending upon whether seasons are cold (grapes become too acid) or hot (grapes overripen). It is on the basis of this figure, and of the legal standards, that the decision to acidify or disacidify is made.

ACIDITY, VOLATILE—In small quantities (from 0.3 to 0.4 gram per liter), excess volatile acids are strictly controlled by law. Only levels below 0.9 gram per liter (production) and 1 gram (retail trade) are tolerated; quantities higher than this make the wine too sour. Volatile acidity, mainly made up of *acetic acid,* increases as the wine ages.

ACIDULATION—Adding acid to wine made from grapes deficient in natural acid in order to bring the wine into balance. It is legal in California (where the warmer climates keep acid levels down), and illegal in France. It's interesting to note that adding sugar (*chaptalization*) is legal in France but illegal in California.

ACRE—An American and British surface measurement equivalent to 4,047 square meters, or 0.4047 *hectares.* There are therefore 2.47 acres in a hectare.

ALCOHOL—An essential element in wine that is produced during fermentation, when enzymes created by the yeasts change the sugar content of the grape juice into alcohol, carbon dioxide, and heat. The level of alcohol in wine varies from under 7 degrees to over 15 degrees. To obtain 1 degree of alcohol, eighteen grams of sugar must be added per liter for white wines, and seventeen grams for red.

AMERICAN VITICULTURAL AREA (AVA)—A grape-growing region recognized as distinct by the BATF. (It is the equivalent of a French *AOC*.) To use an AVA on a wine label, 85 percent of the grapes must come from the appellation.

ANTHOCYANIN—The red pigments in grapes that give red wine its color. The purple-red color of young wine is almost exclusively caused by fairly unstable anthocyanin molecules, which, in the course of aging, join up with *tannins* to change that color to ruby red. This polymerization of tannin and anthocyanin is helped by the dissolution of oxygen in the wine, which produces stable polymers.

AOC (Fr.)—"Appellation d'Origine Contrôlée." This designation was created by the French authorities (the *INAO*) to establish specific areas of production, grape varieties, minimum levels of sugar in the *must* and of alcohol in the wine, maximum yield per *hectare*, pruning of the vine, and cultivation and *vinification* methods.

APPELLATION—The geographic origin of a wine, not synonymous with the term *terroir*.

AROMAS—These are the scents that a wine gives off and that are absorbed by the taster's nose and palate. Three levels of aromas can be distinguished: primary, or varietal, aromas; secondary aromas, resulting from the fermentation; and tertiary aromas, which develop as the wine ages and together form its *bouquet*.

AUSLESE (Ger.)—German white wine made from late-harvest grapes with a high sugar concentration.

BALANCE—The harmony among the various elements of a wine, such as acidity, sweetness, *alcohol*, and *tannin* content.

BALTHAZAR—Mainly used for Champagne, this is a bottle equal to sixteen normal bottles, or 12.8 liters.

BARREL FERMENTED—Wine that is fermented in oak barrels as opposed to stainless-steel tanks.

BARRIQUE (Fr.)—A barrel whose capacity may vary from one region to another: In the Bordeaux area, where it is most commonly used, it contains 225 liters (four *barriques* make one *tonneau*); in the Muscadet area, it contains 228 liters; in Touraine-Anjou, it holds 232 liters. The traditional British equivalent is the hogshead. In France other names are used, depending on the region and capacity; see also PIECE, FOUDRE, QUEUE.

BEERENAUSLESE (Ger.)—*QmP* German wines made from grapes affected by *botrytis cinerea*, or *noble rot*.

BLANC, BLANCO, BRANCO—French, Spanish, and Portuguese, respectively, for "white."

BLANC DE NOIRS—White wine made from red or black grapes.

BLANCS DE BLANCS—"White of Whites"—a white wine made of white grapes, such as a Champagne made of Chardonnay. The term is also used to refer to some wineries' special blends of still white wines, ranging from dry to medium dry.

BLEEDING (Fr. SAIGNÉE)—This process consists of drawing off some of the wine during fermentation; the light-colored wine drawn off is used to make rosé wines (*Clairet* in Bordeaux, and Clarete in Rioja).

BLENDING (Fr. ASSEMBLAGE)—The mixing or "assembling" of several vats of wine varieties to make a more balanced one. This is usually performed after each variety has fermented individually. For example, Bordeaux are usually a blend of Cabernet Sauvignon, Cabernet Franc, and Merlot.

BODEGA (Sp.)—An agricultural estate in Spain. However, wines labeled "bodega" do not necessarily include only grapes from the estate in question.

BODY—This term is used to describe a wine with good *tannic* structure and good aging potential.

BOTRYTIS CINEREA—The famous mold that attacks grapes. It manifests itself either as *gray rot*, which can endanger a harvest, or, in certain atmospheric conditions, as *noble rot*, which is used to make dessert wines such as Sauternes, Barsac, amd Monbazillac; certain Anjou wines; such German wines as Auslese, Beerenauslesen, and Trockenbeerenauslesen; and the famous Hungarian Tokaji.

BOTTLE SICKNESS—Unbalance of wine flavor after bottling or rough travel, caused by excessive aeration; it clears up when the wine is allowed to rest.

BOUCHE (Fr. for "mouth")—The term used to describe the *body* and impressions of a wine when tasting.

BOUQUET—A complex emanation from a wine, perceptible in the nose, resulting from maturation and oak aging. Bouquet is more complex than and encompasses *aroma*, which is present only in young wines. See AROMAS.

BRIX—A measurement of the sugar content of grapes, crucial for determining ripeness and the best time for harvest. Grapes are usually harvested in the range of 20 to 26 degrees brix, depending on the grape variety and the style of wine desired by the winemaker.

BROKER—See COURTIER.

BRUT (Fr.)—For sparkling wines, this term indicates a very low level of sugar (up to fifteen grams per liter); the level is nonexistent in *brut intégral* and *brut zéro* Champagne.

B TONNAGE (Fr.)—The action of stirring the wine in the cask, using a *ton*, or "stick," to stop the lees from falling too quickly under the effects of gravity.

BUDBURST—The stage in the vine's annual cycle when the buds get bigger and open up to expose little green clusters of what will later become grape bunches.

CARBONIC MACERATION—A type of *vinification* during which red wine grapes are put into vats as they are, without being crushed. This used to be a natural process, with the grapes being left to ferment without interference. Now the vat is closed and filled with carbon dioxide, which causes the *malic acid* to break down and intracellular fermentations to take place, changing part of the sugar into alcohol. A few days later the *free-run wine* is drained off to be blended at a later stage with the *press wine*. The alcoholic fermentation is then allowed to finish. This process has proved particularly effective for Gamay wines, such as the Beaujolais *primeurs*, that are sold and consumed when young.

CHAIS (Fr.)—Rooms for vinification, aging, or storage.

CHAPTALIZATION—Named for Chaptal, this well-known technique consists in adding sugar (cane, beet, or rectified and concentrated *must*) to the must before fermentation to give the wines a higher alcoholic content. This technique is strictly forbidden in many countries, and usually controlled by law in those countries that permit it (in France a maximum of three kilos of sugar per hectoliter of grape juice is allowed). New EEC regulations have added to this legislation: Chaptalization should be authorized only under certain conditions relative to the degree of ripeness, the climatic conditions, and the production methods

169

used. Chaptalization is a necessary evil in difficult years; however, in France it has become something of a habit, allowing growers to harvest maximum volume in the sure knowledge that they can boost the degree of alcohol by chaptalizing. The EEC would like French growers to use only rectified, concentrated musts, or RCMs, when chaptalizing. Today, new appliances are used to detect fraudulent chaptalization by nuclear magnetic resonance.

CHÂTEAU—To the northwest of Bordeaux, in the Médoc, most country residences have vineyards that have become famous. As a result, this term has come to designate the wine from a particular estate. A real "château" does not necessarily stand on every property.

CLAIRET (Fr.)—Light red wine obtained by *bleeding* in the course of fermenting red wine. Not to be confused with *claret*, the British way of referring to the red wines of Bordeaux.

CLIMAT (Fr.)—A term originating in Burgundy that indicates a legally defined geographical area; it has nothing to do with weather. However, different *climats* can have varying weather climates within or among themselves.

CLONE, CLONAL SELECTION—In grape nomenclature, the term *clone* refers to a variation, subvariety, or strain that has developed within a given variety of grape; for example, the more than two hundred clones of Pinot Noir. Different clones can produce more grapes or are more resistant to disease, so clonal research has become very important. Until recently, many New World regions practiced *clonal selection*, or deliberately seeking and planting those clones that promise healthier production in order to increase their yields. This practice is becoming less acceptable.

CLONING—A horticultural operation whereby multiplication is obtained from one rootstock only, as opposed to growing a selection of individual stocks.

CLOS (Fr.)—This term originally refered to a vine-growing parcel surrounded by a wall, particularly in Burgundy. Many of the original walls in even the oldest properties are still standing.

COLD STABILIZATION—A method of clarifying wine by lowering its temperature to 32 degrees F for a short period, allowing the suspended particulate matter to drop out.

COMPLEX—The term used to describe a wine that has many different levels and layers of flavors and textures.

CONCENTRATED—The term used to describe a wine that has a lot of extracted matter, and is intense and rich.

CORKED—The expression used for a wine that has a very strong smell of rotten cork. It is usually undrinkable. This rather rare occurrence is caused by the development of certain molds.

COULURE (Fr.)—See SHATTER.

COUPAGE (Fr.)—The term commonly used in Cognac for *blending*.

COURTIER (or BROKER)—The intermediary between the grower and the *négociant*.

CRU (Fr.)—Literally "growth," this term sometimes refers to a tract of land such as a vineyard, but principally to a vineyard's rank in the 1855 classification or ranking of Bordeaux vineyards and their wines into five classes, or crus. Eighty-three Médoc, Graves, and Sauternes châteaux were so classified in 1855, but since then hundreds more around Bordeaux have classified themselves as first to fifth crus, or crus exceptionnels, or crus bourgeois.

CRUSH—The physical act of crushing the grapes; also, the harvest season.

CRUSHER-STEMMER (Fr. ÉGRAPPOIR)—A machine that separates the grapes from the stalks.

CUVAISON (or CUVAGE, both Fr.)—An essential stage in the making of a wine, it takes place from the moment when the *musts* from the harvest are put into the fermentation vats up to the draining off, or *décuvage*.

CUVÉ (Fr.)—A vat designed to hold the fermenting *musts*, or to store wines. Some vats are closed, with an upper lid fitted with a hatch (as in Bordeaux); others are open (as in Burgundy). The vats are made of various materials: Wooden vats were once used, but nowadays stainless-steel vats are preferred for cleanliness and, principally, temperature control.

CUVÉE (Fr.)—Literally "vatful," the word signifies a specific selection of wine that may or may not have been blended (see BLENDING).

DÉBOURBAGE (Fr.)—The operation of pumping off the sediment from the *must* before fermentation.

DECANTING—The process of separating the sediment of a wine from the clear liquid. During the decanting operation a young wine comes into contact with the air, and the addition of oxygen makes it more palatable. Should the wine be too old, this operation can be disastrous, because it accelerates the process of deterioration.

DECLASSIFICATION—When a wine exceeds certain norms for yield, or falls short in degree of alcohol, it is declassified and loses its *Appellation d'Origine Controlée* classification. (The decision may be taken voluntarily.) Such wine may be used to make vinegar or pure alcohol.

DÉCUVAGE (Fr.)—see CUVAISON.

DEPOSIT—The sediment of solid particles found in wine. In the case of white wines, these are often fragments of colorless crystals of tartrate; in red wines, they are usually a combination of *tannins* and pigments. See also DECANTING.

DESSERT WINE—The legal term in America for wines of over 14 percent but not over 24 percent in alcoholic strength by volume; this includes appetizer wines, such as sherries.

DISGORGING (Fr. DÉGORGEMENT)—An important stage in the *méthode champenoise* in which accumulated yeast deposits are eliminated in the course of secondary fermentation in the bottle. See METHODE CHAMPENOISE.

DISTILLATION—The process of separating the alcohol in an alcoholic mixture by heating it, on the principle that alcohol has a boiling point lower than that of water; the first vapors to be given off are alcoholic ones, which can then be condensed by cooling.

DO (Sp.)—"Denominacion de Origen." The Spanish equivalent of the French *AOC*.

DOC (It.)—"Denominazione di Origine Controllata." The Italian equivalent of the French *AOC*. The designation underwrites the origin of the wine, but not necessarily its quality. There are over 220 at present.

DOCE, DOLCE, DULCE—"Sweet" in Portuguese, Italian, and Spanish, respectively.

DOCG (It.)—"Denominazione di Origine Controllata Garantita." This guarantee refers to testing by sensory analysis. Existing designations are Barbaresco, Barolo, Brunello, Chianti, and Vino Nobile di Montepulciano.

DOSING—Once Champagne has undergone *disgorging*, sugar is added to it in the form of *liqueur d'expédition*, which varies depending upon whether the champagne is *brut* (maximum fifteen grams per liter), *extra dry* (from twelve to twenty grams per liter), *sec* (from seventeen to thirty-five grams per liter), or *demisec* (from thirty-three to fifty grams per liter).

EARTHY—A term referring to the positive characteristics of loamy topsoil, mushrooms, or truffles that are sometimes found in red wines.

ÉLEVAGE (Fr.)—Literally "raising," this term describes the operations of maturing and blending young wines to attain better balance.

ENOLOGY, OENOLOGY—The science and study of winemaking.

EN PRIMEUR (Fr.)—Rather than being sold when it is ready to drink, wine is most often offered at a much earlier stage. In Bordeaux the grands crus usually sell all or part of a year's vintage the following March or April, in what are known as sales *en primeur*.

ESPUMOSO, ESPUMANTE—Spanish and Portuguese, respectively, for "sparkling wine," such as Champagne.

ESTATE BOTTLED—This term originally referred to wine produced and bottled entirely at the winery adjoining the proprietor's vineyard, but amendments have broadened it to include vineyards the proprietor controls or that members of a cooperative winery own within the same delimited *viticultural* area as the winery.

ESTERS—Volatile bodies resulting from the combination of an alcohol and an organic acid. They do not have such a marked influence on the wine's bouquet as is commonly thought.

EXTRA DRY—A term describing the quality of sparkling or still wine that contains between twelve and twenty grams of sugar per liter.

FERMENTATION, ALCOHOLIC—The transformation of the sugar contained in the *must* into alcohol and carbon dioxide in the presence of yeasts.

FERMENTATION, MALOLACTIC—This follows the alcoholic fermentation. *Malic acid* is affected by specific bacteria and changed into *lactic acid* and carbon dioxide. Because lactic acid is less harsh than malic acid, the wine becomes softer and more pleasant to drink than when young.

FINING (Fr. COLLAGE)—A way of clearing wines before they are bottled. With this method a colloid is added to the wine to absorb suspended particles, which then fall with gravity to the bottom of the container. Products used are beaten egg white, fish glue, casein, and bentonite, a type of clay. The wine is then drawn off and sometimes filtered before bottling.

FLINTSTONE—A term evoking the smell of two flints being rubbed together. This aroma is characteristic of Pouilly-Fumé from the Loire Valley and some other wines, usually made from the Sauvignon grape.

FLOR (Sp.)—A mold that develops on the surface of a wine in contact with the air; it creates a membrane. It usually has an adverse effect on the taste, but it can be extremely beneficial to certain wines such as sherry. The flor is what gives fino sherry its finesse.

FLOWERING—This essential step in the growing of the grape takes place in the springtime. Early flowering is often considered a portent of a good *vintage*. If the weather is too cold during the flowering period, the grapes may not develop properly (see SHATTER and MILLERANDAGE). The vine is never treated at this stage; its flowers must be impregnated by insects.

FORTIFIED—A term describing a wine to which wine spirit (brandy) has been added, such as port or sherry.

FOUDRE (Fr.)—A large cask with a capacity of two to three hundred hectoliters.

FOURTH LEAF—This term refers to the fourth spring of a young vinestock's existence. From then on it will start to bear wine-producing grapes.

FOXEY—A term describing wines with gamey smells.

FREE-RUN WINE (Fr. VIN DE GOUTTE)—Wine derived from the grape juice before *pressing*, through the natural bursting of the skins.

FROSTS—Winter frosts only affect wine in exceptional circumstances (in more northern vineyards, for example, or in very harsh winters with temperatures of less than 5 degrees F). The most exposed vines during the winter are those at the bottom of valleys, because there is little air circulation. A layer of snow usually protects vineyards from destruction by frosts. On the other hand, spring frosts are sometimes fatal, as they were in 1991, because they kill the growing buds, which are usually full of water and therefore vulnerable. *Flowering* usually takes place at the end of June, when there is no more risk of spring frosts.

FRUITINESS—A characteristic of a young wine, or of a wine that has retained its fruity aromas.

FRUITSET (Fr. NOUAISON)—The stage just after the vine has flowered when the fruit forms.

GLYCERIN—A trialcohol with a slightly sweet flavor, this is one of the important constituents of wine. On the palate it is often more pronounced in wines matured in new oak.

GOBLET (Fr. GOBELET)—A method of pruning the vine in which it takes the shape of a goblet, with several branches coming out of it like horns. Such pruning gives grapes better exposure to the sun.

GRAFTING—After the *phylloxera* crisis, Europe had to use American plants (*Vitis riparia, V. rupestris*) with insect-resistant roots as graft-stock. The European varieties (*V. vinifera*) were then grafted onto these American plants.

GRASSY—A term describing aromas and flavors resembling new-mown grass; these can be a negative characteristic when dominant.

GRAVES (Fr.)—Soils made up of gravels and drift boulders. Also, one of the seven major Bordeaux appellations.

GRAY ROT—See ROT, GRAY.

GREEN—This term refers to a wine with excessive fruit acidity, especially if it has a malic (applelike) aroma.

GROUNDWATER (Fr. NAPPE PHREATIQUE)—The underground layer of water that rises and falls depending on rainfall. Every vinestock has to drink enough water to produce grapes that make good wine. Too much water in the soil and subsoil can be disastrous, but if water is too scarce, the vine cannot survive. Recent surveys have demonstrated that the level of groundwater is of utmost importance to the quality of a wine.

HAIL—An enemy of the vine: Hail damages the bunches, whose stems may break, and the fruits, which, if ripe, may release their juice. Such damage tends to provoke rot and mold.

175

HAUTAIN (Fr.)—A method of pruning the vine upward, often with espaliers, or stakes larger than the standard vine props.

HECTARE—One hundred square meters, the equivalent of 2.47 acres.

HECTOLITER—One hundred liters, the equivalent of 22 imperial or 26.5 U.S. gallons. In the EEC, wine production is referred to in hectoliters per hectare (hl/ha).

HERBACEOUS—This term is used to describe aromas and flavors reminiscent of herbs, or of the leafy and branchy parts of the plant—a negative quality when extreme.

HYBRID—The result of crossing two species of vine. Because of the *phylloxera* crisis and the subsequent crossings of American and European species, phylloxera-resistant hybrids have been produced. Such hybrids have not been encouraged, however, because the quality of the wine has tended to be mediocre.

INAO (Fr.)—The "National Institute of the Appellations d'Origine" is a public body established in France (July 30, 1935) to determine and control the condition of French *Appellation d'Origine Contrôlée* wines. The type of legislation imposed by the INAO has been followed by many countries.

JAMMY—In red wines, this term describes a taste of ripe fruitiness combined with natural berrylike flavors.

KABINETT (Ger.)—Top-end German dry white wines (QmP) that are never chaptalized.

LEES—A dark yellowy deposit at the bottom of a cask that is made up of yeasts in a latent state, *tartaric acid,* and other residual matter from the harvest. Lees are removed during *racking.*

MADEIRIZED—Oxidized or baked, such as by the heat-treatment method practiced in Madeira and some other countries. Also, when a white wine oxidizes badly and browns in color (usually because of poor storage and/or excessive age), it is said to have madeirized. The phenomenon takes its name from the taste of Madeira, and is due to the presence of harmful levels of ethyl aldehyde.

MAGNUM—A large bottle with a capacity of 1.5 liters, or the equivalent of two ordinary bottles. Great wines age more slowly in magnums than in 75-milliliter bottles.

MALIC—A term describing the applelike aroma of *malic acid* from incompletely ripened grapes.

MARC (Fr.)—(1) The solid parts of the grape, obtained after *pressing*, form a cake that is sometimes used for distillation in two different processes: The *marc* can be sprayed with water and drained off before distillation, or it can be placed as it is in special stills into which steam is forced. The resulting spirit is called *eau de vie de marc*, or just *marc* for short. (2) In Champagne, the loading unit for the press, corresponding to four thousand kilos of grapes.

MECHAGE (Fr.)—The process of disinfecting the inside of a cask, barrel, or butt by burning a sulfur wick.

MÉTHODE CHAMPENOISE (Fr.)—The originality of this way of making sparkling wines lies in the creation of effervescence in the bottle. The wines used have completed their fermentations (alcoholic and sometimes malolactic) and are what the Champenois call clear wines; to them is added a *liqueur de tirage* made up of sugar solution and yeasts. The amount of liquid added (about twenty-five grams of sugar per liter) is calculated to obtain a pressure of six atmospheres.

This provokes a second alcoholic fermentation in the bottle, which is carefully closed with a metal capsule (or cork). This second fermentation produces carbon dioxide which is trapped in the bottle and mixes into the wine: That is how the effervescence is formed. The bottles are then stored in a cellar *sur lattes* ("on slats of wood") until they are released onto the market (they can be kept for several years in this way without detracting from their freshness).

When the wines are being prepared for shipping, the deposits of dead yeasts that have fallen by force of gravity to the lower side of the bottle are removed: The operation traditionally involved raising the bottle progressively onto *pupitres* ("racks") and giving it a quarter turn daily (*riddling*) so that the deposit formed against the cork. Today this technique is often replaced by an automatic mechanical operation using "giropallets," which gives excellent results. The bottles come out neck down, and with the deposit collected against the cork. The neck is then immersed in a saline solution, which freezes a few centiliters of the wine, forming a plug of ice that includes the deposit. Next, the capsule is removed in the stage known as

177

dégorgement ("disgorging"). A *liqueur d'expédition* is then added; this is a mixture of old wine, pure spirit (or Cognac), citric acid when necessary, anhydride sulfite, and, most important, a sugar solution in quantities that will determine the designation: *brut* from zero to fifteen grams, *extra dry* from twelve to twenty grams, *sec* from seventeen to thirty-five grams, *demisec* from thirty-three to fifty grams. The bottle can then be corked, wired, and labeled.

METHUSELAH—A 6.4 liter bottle size used for Champagne equivalent to eight normal bottles; also called an *impériale*. Also spelled MATHUSELAH.

MICROCLIMATE—An area where soil, combined with other environmental factors, produces a distinctive wine. This is the more American term for the French *climat*.

MILDEW—A parasitic mold that attacks the green parts of the vine. It used to be treated with copper sulfate, but today synthetic substances are used.

MILLERANDAGE (Fr.)—A partial form of *shatter*. The flowers are pollinated but not impregnated, which means that they do not acquire pips and remain small and green. Uneven development may occur on the same bunch.

MOELLEUX (Fr.)—A term that describes sweet white wines, whose sugar content may vary between twelve and forty-five grams per liter, according to a 1984 EEC directive.

MUSKY—A characteristic of wines made with the Muscatel grape as base, especially during fermentation, when a smell reminiscent of musk is given off.

MUST—Unfermented grape juice obtained by crushing or pressing.

MUTING (Fr. MUTAGE)—This operation involves "fixing" alcoholic fermentation by adding a spirit; it is a characteristic stage in the *vinification* of ports, sherries, and *vins doux naturels*.

NABUCHODONOSOR (Fr.)—A huge bottle, used in Champagne, equivalent to 16 liters, or equal to twenty 750-milliliter bottles.

NATIVE YEAST—Natural yeast attached to the skins of the grapes, sometimes solely used to start the fermentation. If fermentation cannot be started by native, or indigenous, yeasts, then fabricated or synthetic yeasts are used.

NÉGOCIANT (Fr.)—The person who buys wine from the grower or château to sell it to wholesalers or foreign importers.

NÉGOCIANT ELEVEUR (Fr.)—A négociant who first buys wine from grower, then stores the wines in order to mature them, blend them, or both (see ELEVAGE).

NÉGOCIANT MANIPULANT (Fr.)—A trader in Champagne who buys grapes at harvesttime for the preparation of his own Champagne (abbreviated N.M. on the label).

NOBLE ROT—See ROT, NOBLE.

NOUAISON (Fr.)—See FRUITSET.

NOUVEAU (Fr.)—A term describing wine of the most recent *vintage*, which means that after August 31 of the year following the vintage, wines can no longer claim this designation. Beaujolais Nouveau is the classic example. Nowadays an increasing number of wine-producing regions always declare their vintage on the label, but in the regions of Oporto and Champagne the vintage is still declared by the trade in the best years only.

N.V.—Meaning "nonvintage," this designation is used for ports, champagnes, and other wines. Nonvintage wines can also be marketed as V.S.R. ("very special reserve").

OIDIUM—A disease of the vine caused by a microscopic mold that attacks the flowers, leaves, and grapes. The grapes dry out and a whitish dust covers the vine. The only remedy is sulfur treatment.

O.I.V. (Fr.)—The "Office International de la Vigne et du Vin" (International Office of Vine and Wine), established in 1924, carries out studies and investigations on a worldwide scale in technical, economic, scientific, and legal areas.

ORGANOLEPTIC—Smell, color, and taste make up what are called the organoleptic qualities perceived by the senses.

OVERCROPPING—The practice of allowing vines to produce more fruit than they can physiologically ripen.

OXIDATION—When oxygen in the air comes into direct contact with the wine, oxidation may cause changes in color and taste.

OXIDIZED—This term describes a sherrylike, madeirized, or "nutty" flavor caused by the action of oxygen on wine, due mainly to exposure to air, heat, and light.

PASSERILLAGE (Fr.)—Overripening of the grapes at harvest, caus-
ing them to dry out and reach higher sugar levels; this is how
vins de paille, some Muscatels, and the sweet wines of the Juras are
prepared. Not to be confused with the sweet wines obtained as
a result of *noble rot.*

PASTEURIZATION—To "stabilize" low-quality wines and get rid of
any microorganisms, the wine can sometimes be pasteurized, or
heat sterilized like milk.

PERLANT (Fr.)—Said of wines that are very slightly sparkling, but
less so than semisparkling wines.

pH—The measuring unit expressing potential hydrogen, or the concentration of H+ ions. For wines this means their degree of dryness
(between 2.9 and 3.1 for the wines with the best bearing). The
lower the pH, the safer the wine is from disease and *oxidation,* and
therefore the greater its aging potential. See also ACIDITY, REAL.

PHYLLOXERA—This plant louse, imported from the United States,
attacks the vine at its roots, and was the cause of the destruction
of the European vineyards that took place mainly between 1860
and 1880.

PIÈCE (Fr.)—A cask holding 205 liters in Champagne, 214 liters in
Beaujolais, and 216 liters in Mâcon.

PIPE—A cask used for port with a capacity of 523 liters in Oporto, 418
liters in Madeira, 423 liters in Marsala, and 532 liters in Lisbon.

POURRITURE NOBLE—The French term for the *Botrytis cinerea* mold,
literally *noble rot* (*Edelfäule* in German. This mold dehydrates grapes
left late on the vine and concentrates their sweet juice.

PRESSING—The operation whereby the grape juice or wine is produced.

PRESS WINE (Fr. VIN DE PRESSE)—Wine obtained by pressing
the more solid elements that are left in the vat after the draining off of the *free-run wines.* Press wines are sometimes blended
with the free-run wines at a later stage to obtain the best possible balance for the particular vintage in question.

PRIMEURS (Fr.)—Wines designed to be drunk very young enjoy
this designation provided they are marketed between
November 21 and January 31 of the following year. (Not to be
confused with *en primeur.*)

QbA (Ger.)—"Qualitätswein bestimmter Anbaugebeite"—German wines that have been *chaptalized*.

QmP—"Qualitätswein mit Prädikat"—This designation is reserved for German wines of quality that have not been *chaptalized*.

QUEUE (Fr.)—The expression *vin de queue* is used in Sauternes and corresponds to the last picking of grapes. The term also applies to a liquid measure equivalent to twice 228 liters.

QUINTA (Port.)—The Portuguese equivalent of an estate or property. As with *bodegas* in Spain, Quinta wines may come from other properties than the one named.

RACKING (Fr. SOUTIRAGE)—An operation involving separating wine from its *lees* by transferring from one container to another. This aerates and clarifies the wine while leaving the lees and sediment behind in the first container.

RANCIO—There are variations in this term's meaning. In the United States it signifies a pungent taste similar to that of something being cooked in a fortified wine. In France it refers to the character of a Banyuls; in Spain, where the term originated, it is applied to a balance of nuttiness and spirit in a sherry.

RATAFIA—A dessert wine of Champagne and Burgundy, prepared by mixing *marc* brandy and grape juice.

REBECHE (Fr.)—In Champagne, wine obtained from the last part of the *must* after pressing, traditionally by stirring the *marc* with the spades (*bêches*) used for the *taille*. This wine is excluded from the Champagne appellation.

RECIOTO (It.)—A sweet Italian red wine prepared with grapes that have been left for a time on racks, or hung, and which are therefore very concentrated.

RECOLTANT MANIPULANT (Fr.)—A vine grower in the Champagne region who makes his own Champagne (manipulates the grapes).

REFRIGERATION—The physical process used to clarify wines by precipitation of certain solid elements in them.

REMONTAGE—For red wine, the operation of pumping the liquid up from the bottom of the vat and spraying the cap. The object is to achieve optimum contact between the liquid and the sediment of skins, pips, and stalks floating on the top.

181

RESERVE (Fr.)—For wines and spirits, this is the term used for special cuvées put aside for aging or future use. It refers also to a minimum aging period for certain spirits such as Calvados, Cognac, and Armagnac.

RESIDUAL SUGAR (RS)—The level of sugar that remains in wine after fermentation.

RIDDLING (Fr. REMUAGE)—A spectacular as well as basic operation in the *méthode champenoise* involving the collection of deposits of dead yeasts and mineral salts around the cork so as to remove them. This stage is still carried out manually, although giropallets are replacing the *remueur* to an increasing extent.

RIPENESS—A measurement of acid, *pH*, and sugar in the grapes; it is also important in conjunction with the *must*, in order to extract more color and flavor.

ROBE (Fr.)—Literally "dress," this term refers to the overall visual appearance of the wine, including color.

ROGNAGE (Fr.)—The process of pruning the vine shoots to reduce vegetation and reinforce circulation of the sap through the branches.

ROT, GRAY—A rot caused by the same mold as *noble rot*, or *Botrytis cinerea*, which affects grapes damaged by hail or grapeworm. High levels of humidity favor its development. Gray rot affects the quantity of the harvest, alters quality, and can lead to a disease in the wine called oxidasic casse (see CASSE).

ROT, NOBLE—When conditions are favorable—a dry, sunny end to autumn—grapes develop a beneficial form of decay thanks to the development of *Botrytis cinerea*, the celebrated mold that roasts the Sauternes grapes, producing a concentrated, different type of juice.

ROTI (Fr.)—Literally "roasted," a characteristic of sweet wines with aromas of dried grapes resulting from noble rot.

SALMANAZAR (Fr.)—Used in Champagne (9.6 liters).

SEC (Fr.)—Literally "dry"; the word is *secco* in Italian, *seco* in Portuguese and Spanish.

SELECTION BY MASS—The selection of grape varieties coming not from a single clone, but from a group of plants whose genetic structure is different.

SELECTION DE GRAINS NOBLES (Fr.)—"A selection of noble grains." This expression, used particularly in Alsace, may also be used in other regions such as Sauternes, Barsac, Cadillac, Cérons, Loupiac, Ste-Croix-du-Mont, Monbazillac, Bonnezeaux, Quarts de Chaume, Coteaux du Layon, Coteaux de l'Aubance, Jurançon and Graves supérieures. It applies to wines made from late-picked grapes affected by *noble rot*, or from *passerillés* grapes with a natural concentration of sugars.

SEMISPARKLING—The presence of unfermented sugar at the time of bottling gives rise to semisparkling wines; under EEC regulations they are limited to 1 to 2.5 atmospheres of pressure, or 15 to 37.5 pounds per square inch.

SHATTER (Fr. COULURE)—Occurring when the flower is not pollinated, due to bad weather or too early a spring; in shatter the flowers or grapes wither, and develop unevenly or not at all. One of the wine grower's greatest enemies throughout the world. See also MILLERANDAGE.

SORTING (Fr. TRIAGE)—In the course of the harvest, this is the stage during which green or rotten grapes are removed; the term is also used for the successive pickings used in the harvest of *passerillés* grapes or grapes affected by *noble rot*. Finally it can apply to the process of sorting the healthy grapes from the unhealthy, after harvesting, on sorting tables.

SOUR—A fungus (*Mycoderma aceti*) that causes wine to change into vinegar when in contact with air. It develops particularly in inadequately filled vats, giving the wine a sour taste and an extremely unpleasant smell.

SPARKLING—There are several ways of making a sparkling wine: the *méthode champenoise;* what is known as the "rural" method (in Gaillac and Die, for example), when effervescence is the result of a secondary fermentation; and the Charmat or "cuvé close" method. Effervescence may also be produced by adding carbon dioxide. European regulations stipulate that the pressure of sparkling wines must be no less than three atmospheres.

SPÄTLESE (Ger.)—Late-harvested German wines.

STAMPING—The process of marking a wine (on its capsule, cork, crate, or cask) to identify it.

STEMMING—The process of separating the grapes from the stalks. The stalks contain oils and *tannins,* which tend to make the wine bitter and harsh. Thus this process is sometimes needed when the grapes are too soft or lack acidity and structure, because the stems can provide some of the missing body and firmness.

STEMMY—This term describes an unpleasant aroma and taste of wine fermented with an excess use of grapes and stems.

STILL WINES—The opposite of *sparkling* wines. The term also describes wines that are used as a base in the making of sparkling and *semisparkling* wines.

SULFUR DIOXIDE—Winemakers have always used sulfur: It checks premature fermentation in the harvested grapes, destroys undesirable yeasts, eliminates microbes and bacteria, protects oxidation, acts as a dissolving agent, and is a precious ally for sweet white wines inclined to referment in the bottle. Sulfur dioxide is now used either in gaseous form, or diluted in water at 5 or 18 percent. Too much sulfur dioxide can produce a taste of rotten eggs and induces headaches.

SUR LIE (Fr.)—Allowing the wine to be aged in contact with the *lees,* the expired yeast cells from fermentation. This process is usually considered to give the wine more taste and extracts.

TAILLE (Fr.)—(1) The process of pruning the vines' branches in winter with *secateurs* into the shape that will allow them to bear the most fruit, bearing in mind the soil, climate, and grape variety. (2) In Champagne, the part of the *must* that is drawn off by pressing after the *cuvée.* The first and second *tailles* are distinguished.

TANNIN—In English we tend to speak of tannin in the singular; this is inaccurate, because there are different types of tannin, all derived from vegetable substances such as nuts, wood, bark, berries, and, of course, grapes. The stalks, skins, and pips contain tannins, which are released during the fermentation process and the *pressing,* giving the wine its specific character and contributing to its capacity for aging. Storing the wine in new wood allows additional tannin contained in the fibers of the wood to be added.

TART—The sensation of tartness (rough and harsh in the mouth) is caused by excess *tannins.* These are caused by either a rustic grape variety or excessive fermentation.

TERROIR (Fr.)—An all-encompassing French term referring to the particular characteristics of a specific piece of vineyard land, including but not limited to the sum total of soil, exposure, drainage, climate, trellising, and grape variety. More poetically, it is the unique and magic trinity of climate, grape, and soil.

THERMOREGULATION—The process of controlling the temperature of vats during fermentation.

THINNING—A few days before the harvest, it is often helpful to remove the leaves covering the grapes to make the grapes riper and healthier.

TROCKENBEERENAUSLESE (Ger.)—Very sweet German wine of the QmP type: the top of the range in its category.

TUN—The British measure equivalent to a cask of 210 gallons, or 955 liters.

ULLAGE—The vacant area in a bottle or cask between the wine and the cork or roof of the cask. Bottle ullage increases with time, because the wine breathes through the cork. Always look out for excessive ullage when buying an older wine.

185

VARIETAL (Fr. VIN DE CÉPAGE)—(1) Wine made from a single grape variety. In France the wine must contain 100 percent of the same variety; in some other countries small proportions of other varieties are allowed, and in still others there is no relevant regulation. (2) Said of wine having the pronounced aroma and flavor of a grape variety. This is also the general term for wines labeled with names of grape varieties.

VATROOM (Fr. CUVIER)—Where the vats or cuvés are kept.

VENDANGES TARDIVES (Fr.)—"Late harvesting," which is done to procure overripe grapes for sweet wines.

VERAISON (Fr.)—The stage in the ripening of the grape when the fruit changes color.

VIN CLAIR (Fr.)—The name given in Champagne to still white wines before the second fermentation is introduced by the méthode champenoise.

VIN DE GOUTTE (Fr.)—See FREE-RUN WINE.

VIN DE PRESSE (Fr.)—See PRESS WINE.

VINICULTURE—The science or study of grape production for wine and of the making of wine.

VINS SUR LATTES (Fr.)—Wines that have been made into Champagne and are stockpiled on their *lees* prior to *riddling*.

VINTAGE—Originally this term referred to the grape harvest; because there is only one per year, though, the term has come to refer to the wine made from the harvest of a particular year. Each vintage acquires its specific nature from a combination of climatic factors that determine the wine's quality and potential for aging.

The differences in quality from one year to another are such that most *négociants* blend wines from different vintages to create a better-balanced product. The outstanding vintages deserve to stand on their own, however, so they are kept as single-harvest stock to be made available as vintages. In the past such vintages were very rare, and wines were sold as *N.V.* ("non-vintage") or V.S.R. ("very special reserve").

VITICULTURE—The cultivation, science, and study of grapes.

INDEX

"accessible" wines, 17
accolage, 54
acetate, 33
acidity, 24–25, 27, 34, 39, 48, 56, 60, 66
acids, 151, 154, 158
aeration, 125, 149, 150
aging, 23–42
alcohol content, 7, 9, 10, 23–24, 28, 43, 51, 66, 67, 155
Alsace (French region), 105
Alsace (wine)
    glasses for, 140
    for starter cellar, 96
amidon, 34
amphorae, 6, 9, 10–13, *12*
anthocyanins, 25, 26, 33, 64
apogee, 134
appellations, 47, 152
Argentina, wines of, 83
Armenia, wines of, 6
aromas, 32, *66*, 142, 153–54
    decanting and, 149
    tasting vocabulary of, 159
astringency, 26, 31, 34
Aszú, 40–41
auctions, 21, 100–3
Auslese, 42
Australia, wines of, 28, 44, 71, 73, 76, 80, 91

Bacchus, 5
balance, 48, 56, 151
barrel aging, 32, 36
Beaujolais Nouveau, 41, 52, 142
beer, 11
Beerenauslese, 42
Beverage Buyer, 103
Beverage Media, 97, 103
Bible, wine in, 5, 8
BIVB (Bureau Interprofessionnel des Vins de Bourgogne), 55
"body," 24, 26
Bordeaux (French region), 14, 17, 28, 108
Bordeaux (wine)
    generic, 71
    glasses for, 140
    red, 89–90
    size range of bottles, 134–35
    for starter cellar, 95
    white, 90
Botrytis cinerea, 41
botrytized wine, 28, 41
bottle aging, 32–33, 33*t*, 36, 153
bottles, 12, 134
    opening, 145–48
    organization of, 132–38
bouchonné, 147
bouquet, 33, 153–54
Bourgogne, 140

Brillat-Savarin, Anthelme, 5
brokers de place, 108
bubbles, 27, 140, 147, 152
budburst, 49, 51
Burgundy (French region), 45, 62–69
Burgundy (wine)
  red, 90
  serving temperature, 142
  for starter cellar, 96
  white, 90
"butterfly" corkscrews, 146

Cabernet Sauvignon, 45, 92
  American, 78–79, 82–83, 94
  Australian, 73, 76, 80
  Chilean, 74, 76, 80, 95
  generic, 71
  grapes, 47
  Portuguese, 78
Caecubus wine, 9
Caesar, Julius, 11
California, wines of, 44, 93
  Central Coast, 61–62
  harvest report, 56, 57t, 58–62
  Mendocino County, 59
  Monterey region, 61
  Napa Valley, 59
  Sierra Foothills region, 60
  Sonoma, 59
Campania (Italy), 9
cane burning, 52–53
catalogues, 100, 102
Cato, 7
cave, 1, 2, 14–15, 122
  temperature of, 144, 145
cellar books, 135, 136–37, 138
cellaring, 2, 36, 119–22
  alternatives to, 125–32
  ideal storage conditions, 122–25
  weather conditions and, 102–3
  wines to choose for, 70–83
Chablis, 65–66, 81
chain wine stores, 98–99
chais, 4
chambré, 142, 144
Champagne (French region), 105
Champagne (wine), 29, 113
  food pairings with, 157–58
  glasses for, 140, 147
  opening a bottle of, 146–47
chaptalization, 56, 66, 114
Chardonnay, 45
  American, 73, 75, 78, 94, 95
  Australian, 71, 73, 76, 95

Chardonnay (*cont.*)
  Chilean, 71–72, 74
  grapes, 47, 59, 61, 63, 65, 157
  Italian, 72, 74
  Portuguese, 72
charts, 43–44, 46, 134
châteaux, 14, 40, 105, 107–8, 111, 119, 128
  corks of, 147
Chianti, 72, 75, 77, 95
Chile, wines of, 44, 71–72, 74, 76, 80
chilling, 144, 147
cigars, wine and, 141
climate regions, 47–48, 71
Cognac, 140, 141
collections, 1–5, 118
  organizing, 132–38
  "ready-to-drink" sample cellar, 89–91
  starting, 92–96
  vintage charts and, 44
collectors, 19–21
colloids, 34
color, 25, 26, 33
complexity, 48
consumer bottle aging, 3–4
containers. *See* amphorae; bottles; tonneaux
corks, 121, 145–47
corkscrews, 145–46
cost, 87–89, 98, 103, 106
  en primeur system and, 107–12
Côte du Rhône (French region), 96
Crémant d'Alsace, 28
Crémant de Bourgogne, 28
critics, 18, 111
cultural identity, wine and, 15
customs regulations, 106–7
cuvaison, 31

débourrement, 49, 51t
decanting, 148–51
dégustation, 19
deposits, 148–50
dilation, 120
Diocletian, 8
Dionysus, 5
direct buying, 104–7
"disk," 26, 152
Dovaz, Michel, 115
dryness, 24, 28, 34
ducted storage system, 130

Egypt (ancient), wine in, 6, 7

188

Eiswein, 42
élevage, 54
Enotria, 6
en primeur, buying, 100, 107–12, 113, 118
environment
    for serving wine, 139–40
    winemaking and, 48–49
esters, 25, 27, 34
etiquette, 41–142
exogene tannins, 25–26

Falernum vineyard, 9
false maturity, 47–48
fermentation, 24–25, 29–32, 30–31, 34, 53
    aromas from, 153
    manipulation of, 52
fertilizers, 53
"finale," 155
floraison, 49, 50, 51t
flowering, 49
food, wine and, 15–16, 156–58
formaldehyde, 33
fortified wines, 28, 144
fragrance. See aromas; bouquet
France, wines of, 6, 36, 62–69, 72, 74, 76–77, 80–81. See also names of French regions
    for starter cellar, 95–96
frosts, 49, 50, 51, 52, 54
fruits, 34, 36, 151
fumatoires, 13

Gamay grapes, 67
Gaul, wine in, 11–12
gelatin, 34
Germany, wines of, 28, 41–42, 77, 81
Gewurztraminer grapes, 59
globalization, wine and, 4–5, 16–17, 39
grafting, 53
grapes, 29, 38, 151, 152. See also specific grape names
    acidity of, 24
    aroma of, 153
    seasonal cultivation of, 52–55
    wild, 6
gray rot, 64, 66, 68
great wines, 37–42
Greece, wines of, 29, 83
Greece (ancient), wine in, 6–8, 14, 39
gris wines, 71
Gruaud-Larose, 35

Guide de la Cave, 45

hail, 50, 67
hang time, 48
Harnois, Georges, 130, 131
harvesting, 49, 54–55
harvest reports, 55–56, 57t, 58–62
    analyzing vintages, 62–69
heritage, 48–49
hilling up, 52
home, buying from, 106–7
humidity, 102, 103, 121, 123–24, 130–32, 133
Hungary, wines of, 28, 40–41, 83

importing companies, 93
inexpensive (ready-to-drink) wines
    Australia, 71
    Chile, 71–72
    France, 72
    Italy, 72
    Portugal, 72
    quantity to buy, 85
    United States, 73
insulation, 121–22, 126
investments, 93
investors, 19–21
Italy, wines of, 5–6, 9, 12, 14, 28, 72, 74–77, 81–82

Johnson, Hugh, 84
Jura (French region), 28

Kabinett, 42

labels
    humidity and, 121, 123, 133
    reading, 110
lactic acid, 24
Languedoc-Roussillon (French region), 96
Latour, 35
"laying down," 2
Lebanon, wines of, 83
lees, 30
"legs," 24, 26, 153
light, effect on wine, 99–100, 120, 124, 126
limited-edition wines, 20
Liqueur Muscat, 28
livre de cave, 135
Livre d'Or (Dovaz), 115
Loire Valley (French region), 28, 96, 105

long-term wines
  Australia, 80
  Chile, 80
  France, 80–81
  Germany, 81
  Italy, 81–82
  Portugal, 82
  quantity to buy, 86
  Spain, 82
  for starter cellar, 93–94
  United States, 82–83
lora, 7

Madeira, 32
"madeirized" wines, 158
magnums, 134
malic acids, 24–25, 34
malolactic fermentation, 24–25, 30–31,
  34, 53
maturation, 32–37, 35t, 134
  beginning of, 54
  decanting and, 148
  false maturity, 47–48
mead, 11
medium-term wines
  Australia, 76
  Chile, 76
  France, 76–77
  Germany, 77
  Italy, 77–78
  Portugal, 78
  quantity to buy, 86
  Spain, 78
  for starter cellar, 94
  United States, 78–79
mercator, 12
Merlot, 45
  American, 75, 78
  Australian, 71
  Chilean, 72, 74
  grapes, 61
mers, 34
Meursault (French region), 45
Middle Ages, wine in, 9
mildew, 50, 54, 63, 64
millerandage, 50
Mini Cellar, 131
mold, 121, 147
Muscadet, 41
must, 13, 30

Napa Valley (California), 56, 57t, 58, 59
Narbonne (France), 6, 14
négociants, 105, 107

new wines, 8–9, 17
New Zealand, wines of, 83
noble rot, 41–42

oidium, 54
Opimian wine, 9
oxidation, 32, 33, 142, 147, 158
oxyreduction, 34

parasites, 51, 54
Parker, Robert, 44
pH, 24, 60
phylloxera, 53
Physiologie du goût, La (Brillat-Savarin), 5
Pinot Meunier grapes, 29, 157
Pinot Noir
  American, 82, 94
  grapes, 29, 47, 61, 62, 63, 64–65,
    66–67, 157
  serving temperature, 142
piquette, 7
Pliny, 9
Pliny the Elder, 11
polymerization, 34
polyphenols, 25, 33
Pompeii, wine cellars of, 14
port, 10, 28, 32, 91, 113
Portugal, wines of, 28, 29, 72, 75, 78,
  82
posca, 7
première bouche, 154
première tranche, 109, 111
Prosecco, 28
Provence (French region), 96
pruning, 52, 53

Qualitätswein, 42
quintas, 29

racking, 30
rain, 50, 57t, 58, 61, 63, 64
Rakoczi family, 40
ratings, 44
ready-made cellars, 129–32
red wines, 28, 41
  acidity of, 24–25
  decanting of, 150–51
  fermentation of, 29, 30, 31–32
  food pairings with, 157
  long-term, 93–94
  medium-term, 94
  pigmentation of, 25
  quantity to buy, 85–86
  serving temperature, 143–44